From Illiteracy To The White House

Rod Williams

From Illiteracy To The White House

Author's Note

What you read in this book is true, recounted at best from my memory. Much of the dialogue has been reconstructed, but in essence accurate to the best of my recall.

Writing this book became an emotional experience for me. You too may experience the emotion with my expression of events as I conquered not only my illiteracy, but the stigma of being considered a retarded person.

My saboteur was my First Grade Life Agreement. I had to destroy the saboteur in order to defeat illiteracy and convince first myself and then others that I was a person of intelligence and success.

Today the ugly war of illiteracy remains real and continues to haunt too many.

Opportunity

They do me wrong who say I come no more
When once I knock and fail to find you in;
For every day I stand outside your door
And bid you wake, and rise to fight and win.

Wail not for precious chances passed away!
Weep not for golden ages on the wane!
Each night I burn the records of the day—
At sunrise every soul is born again!

Dost thou behold thy lost youth all aghast?
Dost reel from righteous Retribution's blow?
Then turn from blotted archives of the past
And find the future's pages white as snow.

Art thou a mourner? Rouse thee from thy spell;
Art thou a sinner? Sins may be forgiven;
Each morning gives thee wings to flee from hell,
Each night a star to guide thy feet to heaven.

Laugh like a boy at splendors that have sped,
To vanished joys be blind and deaf and dumb;
My judgments seal the dead past with its dead,
But never bind a moment yet to come.

Though deep in mire, wring not your hands and weep;
I lend my arm to all who say "I CAN!"
No shame-faced outcast ever sank so deep
But yet might rise and be again a man!

Walter Malone (1866–1915)
(Rittenhouse)

Contents

Table of Images

Foreword

1946 logging town, north of
Jump-off Joe, Oregon Coast

It was a beautiful fall morning, a wonderful time to stroll the wooden walkways overlooking the pounding surf left from the previous night's storm. World War II was over, and I was looking forward to my husband returning from Europe and resettling in Portland. My good friend had asked me if I would watch her five-year-old daughter, Kimberly, so that she could visit with her sister. We strolled hand in hand—me, Kimberly, my four-year-old son, Rodney, enjoying the beautiful morning in this small, rugged logging community.

The roadside was littered with rough-hewn cedar plank picnic tables and benches. Hovering over them, the cedar, hemlock, and Douglas fir trees were dwarfed and bent from many years of winter storms that blew in off the Pacific Ocean. Small buildings built of cedar shingles were haphazardly placed along the town road where they could gain the most protection from driving ocean weather.

The children and I, hungry for breakfast, entered a corner diner overlooking the ocean. Inside we saw a wooden counter with rustic bar stools that looked locally

1

made. Three burly loggers sat at the counter having their morning coffee. I ushered the children to the right where we took a booth, seating Rodney next to me by the window and Kimberly across from us with her back to the door. A waitress greeted us with a sweet smile and took our order.

A man walked in who appeared to be another logger. I saw a flash of light next to me and the explosions of a handgun, firing two shots. Kimberly screamed and shot over the table to get to my side, wetting her pants on the way.

To my utter amazement, Rodney jumped to his feet on the bench. Using his hands like a toy gun, he pointed at the man and yelled, "Bang! Bang!"

I grabbed my son to make him stop, terrified that the man would turn on us. The men at the counter quickly subdued the gunman and took him out of the diner. Poor Kimberly couldn't stop crying. The waitress brought us our order with trembling hands. Rodney, on the other hand, was not the least bit upset over the incident and ate his breakfast with gusto.

As I watched him, I couldn't help but be amazed at his fearless approach to what had just happened. Little did I know that this four-year-old who had jumped to my rescue would twenty-two years later be using the same bravado to meet any challenge, including those in the White House.

-- Laura Read (my mother)

Introduction

A student once asked his Rabbi, "Why did God create man?" The Rabbi said, "Because God wished to behold himself."

Why would I write my own story? I write it because I wish to behold myself. I wish to understand how the impossible becomes the possible.

On the banks of a river, several people notice a child floundering in the water, about to drown. None of the observers on the bank can swim. One scrawny young man jumps into the water to save the child, and though he is unable to swim, he struggles to stay afloat. Murmurs arise among the onlookers. "What a fool!" one says. "Now two will drown!" says another. The man fights and struggles with every ounce of courage he has. He finally reaches the floundering child, both now about to drown. A voice, unheard by everyone but the foolish man, commands him on, and he comes alive, secures the child, and with great effort, struggles toward the shore. Upon reaching the banks of the river, the observers help him and the child out of the river. With the child secure in the arms of the mother, all attention is directed to the foolish rescuer.

How did the one who could not swim save the child? "It's a miracle!" The people put their arms around the man and proclaim him a hero. "There, at least at the beginning, the hero is never particularly courageous, strong, gallant, or skillful. Far from it, he is always the youngest, the idiot, the fool. But interestingly enough, it is precisely this 'simpleton' who succeeds in accomplishing the great work" (Banzahaf). Welcome to a fool's journey.

What did my teachers say about me? Did they talk about me as a weak-minded, naive simpleton trying but not able to learn? Maybe one would say, "He putters aimlessly through class, wastes time." Did they see past this to say, "It is difficult for him to express himself, but I find him adventurous with an open curiosity and desire to learn"?

When I was a child, my mother gave me a gift that, along with a strong will, became a tool I clung to with tenacity to overcome the obstacles that life would throw my way. That gift was the nursery rhymes she read to me night after night from The Child's World, a book I have to this day. It is now tattered and worn, but the rhymes it contains have been my constant companion. I memorized every rhyme in the book. I became the characters: Bye Baby Bunting, Little Boy Blue, Simple Simon, and Paul Bunyan.

Although the pictures and stories lived in my mind, I could not read the words on the page. My family moved time after time, and I moved from school to school. I "fell through the cracks," and the gift of reading eluded me.

I went through school with the hidden malady of illiteracy at a time when "leaving a child behind" was commonplace. I was branded as retarded and destined to become one of the future "ditch diggers" of America. I accepted this branding without question.

Even still, my imagination soared with the pictures in the book and stories from which my mother read. I relied on her to read to me, and as I grew, the rhymes became the prose that helped me to conquer illiteracy.

Despite wanting badly to disappear from society, the tenacity I was endowed with was ultimately my key to overcoming my handicap.

Four-year-olds are not supposed to stand up to gunmen, and simpletons are not supposed to know something the teacher doesn't. Illiterates are not supposed to write books, and ditch diggers are not supposed to put arrogant politicians up against the wall in the White House.

1
My First-Grade Life Agreement

I was six years old on my first day of grade school. There were about fifteen of us, all scared students, all pretty much at the same educational level, although some may have been slightly further along than others. It's fair to say that the day was not for learning reading, writing, and arithmetic but to just survive.

It was a day of dealing with the anxiety of separation and the unknown. "Will I catch the right bus home? Who is this strange lady Mommy said would be my teacher? Who are all these strange faces?" I thought as I timidly slid into my desk with its scratches and carved attempts at graffiti.

I survived the first day well. A few days later, when I was introduced to the Dick and Jane reader, my teacher, a petite, young lady with long, dark-brown hair, realized that I could not properly pronounce words. My parents learned from our family dentist that I was born with an unusually high palate (the roof of my mouth was abnormally high), which affected my speech. I stuttered as well, creating a serious challenge for my teacher. I adapted and spoke only when I absolutely had to.

I was held back my first year of school, and not passing the first grade was the beginning of many blows. I acquired a nervous habit of chewing on my shirt collar.

In 1948–1949, we lived in the outskirts of Portland, Oregon. When my father returned from the second World War, he went to work as a mechanic for Hoffman Construction. Dad had wrestled in high school and later became the Pacific Northwest wrestling champion with the Multnomah Athletic Club. He was a tough disciplinarian, a sad victim of learned behavior from his father and grandfather, and he enforced his will liberally upon his oldest son—me. I was a sensitive child, difficult to understand and easily disturbed. My maternal grandfather, who I called "Bop," understood this. My father, on the other hand, did not and set out to mold me into the son he thought I should be.

My mother raised me to be a good Irish lad, and she is best described with the words of the poet Strickland Gillilan:

> You may have tangible wealth untold;
> Caskets of jewels and coffers of gold,
> Richer than I you can never be,
> For I had a mother who read to me.
> *(Gillilan)*

Because of Mom's love for books, my parents purchased two sets of books: My Book House in Twelve Volumes and The Child's World in Six Volumes. We had no TV, and it rained a lot. Sitting next to my mother on rainy days and evenings, I digested the illustrated pictures as she read Mother Goose nursery rhymes and stories to me. I realized many years later that listening to my mother read was both a bonding experience and pure learning delight. By the time I was in the third grade, I had memorized more than thirty-six Mother Goose nursery rhymes in the order that they were illustrated in volume one of The Child's World and was familiar with many more. My favorite was Simple Simon, trying to catch a whale. He became my alter ego.

*Simple Simon went a fishing
for to catch a whale
But all the water he could find
was in his mother's pail.*
(Bjoland 1950)

Image 1 Simple Simon

One of my earliest memories was fishing in the tide pools on the Oregon coast in the early 1940s while World War II raged. My father was in Europe, fighting under General Patton. My Mom and her best friend, Aunt Helen who was married to Dad's older brother Chuck, stationed in the South Pacific with the Navy CB's (Construction Battalion) decided to share a beachfront cottage in Newport, Oregon. Mom and Aunt Helen often took Jerry, my cousin, and me to the beach to play at low tide.

Mom showed me a picture of a whale and told me that it was the largest of all the creatures in the ocean. She sat me next to a small tide pool, and I watched the tiny fish, trapped because of the low tide, dart about. She made me

a fishing pole with a stick, string, and some bright-colored yarn. With my fishing pole, I pretended that the little fish were whales and that I was going to catch one.

During the summer after my first grade year, I went fishing with my Grandpa on the banks of the Colombia River on Sauvie Island. I hooked a big buck salmon and was almost pulled into the river because of his size.

Image 2 My first King Salmon - I hooked him, Grandpa landed him.

Grandpa saved the day—he took hold of my pole, set the hook, and reeled the big fish in, allowing me to help hold the pole. I pretended that I had caught my first whale.

I got to spend a lot of time with my grandparents in Saint Johns that summer, after which we moved closer to Portland and lived in a house on Missouri Street. My younger brother and two younger sisters later referred to it as "the big white house," and it was big compared to what we had lived in before.

Moving during the summer meant that I would attend a new school to repeat the first grade. At Rose Elementary School, white-haired Mrs. White was my first grade teacher, and here came the Dick and Jane reader all over again. As hard as I tried, my struggle to learn to read and write was futile.

By the end of the year, Mrs. White pushed me to the second grade but made a note on my report card that while I had marks of S for Satisfactory, "He still is not reading with the first grade…His absences have *retarded* him." Maybe she meant that my cognitive skills were not adequate for my environment and that I needed extra attention.

However, there was no follow-up, and my parents were left to decide what the comment meant. For Mrs. White to use the word *retarded* was disastrous; they interpreted it to mean that I was slow, and worse, dumb. In 1940s and 1950s America, it was not the norm to question a teacher's evaluation, especially for working-class parents.

TEACHER'S COMMENTS

Date: **MAR 28 1950**

Rodney seems to be
more interested in school.
I hope he will be able to
attend more regularly.

Sincerely yours, *Nellie M. White*

Date: **JUN 9 1950**

While Rodney has marks
of "S" he still is not reading
with the first grade. He
should read some library
books during the summer.
His absences have retarded him.
Sincerely yours, *Nellie M. White*

Days Present	17½	35	38	57½
Days Absent	2	6	7	11½
Times Tardy	0	0	0	0

School Year: Sept. 19**49** to June 19**50**

Assigned to **Second Grade**

FARENTS COMMENTS

First Period:

Parent's Signature

Second Period:

Parent's Signature

Third Period:

Parent's Signature

To Parents

This pupil progress report is sent home four times a
year to inform you of the progress your child is making
in the varied activities of the school. All marks are
given in terms of the individual child's ability to succeed.

If the child is to progress with his class, you
will be invited to confer with his teacher.

You are welcome to call the school for a conference
with the teacher or principal for further information
about your child.

_____ Principal

Image 3 My second year in the first grade and the beginning of my First Grade Life Agreement

12

I realized later that in the post-World War II era, many educators followed a meritorious system of education, enforced by prominent educators who believed that boys such as me were a burden on the school system. We were not to be rewarded but guided to lower-class employment. We were seen as "the future ditch-diggers of America," a phrase used liberally to identify lower-class, male workers.

Voltaire stated, "The lower classes should be guided, not educated" (Aires, 311). This idea was reinforced by Dr. John L. Tildsley of the New York public school system in his Ingles lecture at Harvard University, titled "The Mounting Waste of the American Secondary School." "The stream into the high schools of pupils from the grammar schools who are not equipped with brains or aptitudes for a high-school education is a cause of waste and tremendous expense. This is not only in the money expended to care for them, but in the sacrifice of time of the abler pupils" (Tildsley). Tildsley suggested that the great stream be classified and subdivided and the different streams directed to occupations or studies adapted to their abilities.

This philosophy became the foundation of my First-Grade Life Agreement.

Aristotle reasoned that if a person was deaf and could not use his voice as hearing people do, he was unable to learn and develop on a level equal to the rest of society (Aristotle). Over time, if he was silent, had a stutter or another speech disorder that rendered him unable to be understood, he was classified as "dumb."

In 1948, this thinking prevailed. If you couldn't speak, you were dumb. I knew this to be true, because my father told me many times. The last time he told me that I was retarded or slow was when I was twenty-three. A few years before that, my uncle helped me to get a job, and in comparing me with a stepbrother, my father said that because of my retardation, I would always need help finding work. Little did he realize that six years later, his son would be employed by the most elite service organization in the world.

I am the master of my words
I create them
Whether written or spoken
I carry the power to judge them
To cast out those that would do harm
To reward those that would do well
With this awesome force and power
That my words give me
I must remember
I am held responsible
For my words
To my God!

2
Bad Thing

The summer following my second year in the first grade, my mother worked with me as best she could. She read those familiar nursery rhymes and stories to me over and over. At home, I was still viewed as slow. Outside the family, the name-calling was affecting my self-esteem. To overcome this, I escaped to my bedroom to be by myself, where I opened my nursery rhyme books that my mother had read to me so often. Over time, the nursery rhyme characters had became my imaginary friends that I talked to and played with. They always understood me, and I felt better because of it.

My father became my speech therapist. He scuffed me alongside my head with the palm of his calloused hand when I didn't pronounce my words correctly or when he couldn't understand me. When I acted up, he went to the bathroom and got Bad Thing, a name that I had given his razor strap. Bad Thing had complete command of the bathroom; a big brass snap at the top of its head allowed it to hang from its perch next to the sink and intimidate me with its penetrating stare. Bad Thing was four inches wide, a quarter inch thick, and more than a foot long. I told my imaginary friends not to tell anyone that I was afraid of it. I often skipped brushing my teeth and went to the bathroom in the backyard to avoid it. My dad used Bad Thing to sharpen his straight razor before shaving but also to hit me. He and Bad Thing seemed to be good friends.

At school, I was often teased and referred to as Simple Simon, a name that I identified with. I withdrew into myself, avoiding my father and my peers at school as best I could, and I found comfort in being alone, left to create my own imaginary world. For the next twenty years, my life was ruled by the judgment and sentence that became my First-Grade Life Agreement. *They say I am retarded, so I guess I am.*

The second grade brought writing and arithmetic. I still could not pronounce words clearly, and I was not able to learn the phonetic value of letters, letter groups, or syllables. I could not spell or write in any organized way and had trouble understanding basic arithmetic. In the second grade, I received straight Fs. My First-Grade Life Agreement had now received support units for its foundation.

As a boy, I was blessed with a vivid imagination that I often called on to entertain myself. The more my self-esteem broke down, the more I withdrew into my imagination. I had created a host of secret, imaginary friends. One day, my secret friends and I attempted to make an agreement with Bad Thing that as long as I remained retarded, like Simple Simon, it would not hit me. I kept my agreement with Bad Thing and remained retarded and continued to stutter. Bad Thing didn't keep his agreement though, and with the help of my dad, he continued to hurt me. There were times when I had to stay home from school because of the welts on my legs.

I was pushed to the third grade along with a ball and chain of low self-esteem. Outside the home, I was socially unconnected and reverted to showing up at school and just passing time. I longed for the evenings when I could look at the comic books my mother bought for me. At that time, GI Joe, Hopalong Cassidy, and Red Rider were my favorites, and I looked at the pictures and imagined the stories.

That spring, something happened in the apple tree outside my bedroom window that ignited a desire to explore and learn as much as I could. My motivation was inspired by a story my mother read to me called "The Secret":

We have a secret, just we three,
The robin, and I, and the sweet cherry tree;
The bird told the tree, and the tree told me,
And nobody knows it but just we three.

But of course, the robin knows best,
Because he built the—I shan't tell the rest;
And laid the four little—something in it—
I'm afraid I shall tell it every minute.

But if the tree and the robin don't peep,
I'll try my best the secret to keep;
Though I know when the little birds fly about
Then the whole secret will be out.

(Bjoland, 45)

I came alive with an unquenchable desire to learn and understand all that I possibly could about two robins building a nest in the upper branches of that apple tree. After the nest was built, they laid five speckled eggs. My bedroom window offered an excellent view of all that was happening, and I sat and watched the mother sit on her clutch of eggs day after day until they hatched. It was like an open theater—as soon as I got home from school, I rushed upstairs and watched the baby robins.

On weekends, I got up when the sun was beginning to rise and the dew was still on the ground and hurried outside to observe the robins harvesting worms from the neighboring lawns. I then rushed upstairs and spent as much of the day as possible watching my robin's nest, studying the chicks' every move, and timed the coming and going of the parents.

The weaker chicks were pushed out of the nest, and only two survived. I learned that if I were to survive, I would have to be "one of the strong ones."

My inability to pronounce words correctly, along with my stuttering, made it about impossible to be understood. The black board was a foreign language. When cursive writing was introduced, you might as well have written in Arabic. The only thing I learned from the blackboard that year was how to clean erasers after school.

At home, Bad Thing hit me more often than ever before, and I couldn't understand why. I believed I was being good. I flinched at the very presence of Bad Thing and my dad. I was dumb, retarded—why wouldn't Bad

Thing and my dad leave me alone? I envied other kids who were whipped with their dad's belt or an open hand.

As I matured, I realized that Bad Thing was powerless without my dad. With the help of my secret friends, we devised a plan: by getting rid of Bad Thing, my dad would resort to some other type of instrument, and anything would be better than Bad Thing.

The opportunity came one spring day when I found myself at home with only my secret friends. We were in the bathroom, and Bad Thing stared at me and told me that when dad got home, he would get to hit me. I told Bad Thing, "*No*, you will never hit me again!" Though my speech was impaired, I did not stutter.

I grabbed Bad Thing by his big brass snap, unhooked him, and lifted him up, holding him tightly. "See, Bad Thing, in my hand, you have no power to hurt me. You are nothing but a dumb, stupid moron. At least I can speak out loud and you can't. You're just a stupid retard, that's all you are, a *retard*." I yelled the last word as loud as I could.

With Bad Thing secure in my hands, a strange power come over me. I imagined my dad kneeling on the bathroom floor in front of me, and with the encouragement of my secret friends and my newfound power, I began to beat him. Gripping it with both hands, I swung Bad Thing over and over with all my might, hearing it slap and pop on my dad's imaginary buttocks. I screamed, "See, Bad Thing, now you get to hurt my daddy like you hurt me!"

I swung until I collapsed to the bathroom floor, leaning against the wall, sobbing and shaking, tears rolling down my cheeks. "I'm sorry, Daddy, I'm so sorry, I love you so much."

The image of my dad was gone, my secret friends were gone, and I was alone on the bathroom floor, holding Bad Thing in my hands. At that moment, Bad Thing became just a razor strap, not something that would ever be used again to beat me. I hid it in Mom and Dad's bedroom closet. I remember, as if it were yesterday, my unshaven father standing on the front porch on a sunny, Sunday morning, asking me where his razor strap was. I said that I didn't know and peddled my bicycle up the sidewalk. I never saw Bad Thing again.

I later learned from my mom that Dad talked about how his father whipped him with a razor strap and that "what was good for him would be good for me." My mother also told me my father bragged about how he got back at his father by hiding his razor strap much the same as I hid his.

I wonder if my father stopped whipping me with his razor strap after I hid it because he realized that I had done exactly what he had. This may have played a part in bringing him to realize the magnitude of his own physical abuse. I later learned that my mom had gone to my dad's mother to complain about his physical abuse, and my grandmother passed this information on to my Uncle Chuck, my dad's older brother. He started working with my dad to improve our relationship, and Dad began showing much more interest in me.

My Uncle Chuck was a hard disciplinarian, but the difference between the brothers was the type of discipline. Uncle Chuck administered hard work or, as he said in military fashion, "extra duty" and other creative, on-the-spot punishments.

For example, one day, when visiting Uncle Chuck at his farm near Redland, Oregon, all the kids from the two families were getting our picture taken on the back of Dick, a large draft horse. When we were somewhat securely arranged for the photo shoot, my cousin, Tim, decided to kick Dick in the ribs with his heels. Dick jumped, and we all fell off except Tim, who held onto Dick's mane with both hands and a mischievous grin. Aunt Helen hollered, "Timothy Williams, I saw that!"

The commotion brought Uncle Chuck and my dad out of the farmhouse. Uncle Chuck reigned in Dick, chewed Tim out, and instructed his mischievous son to fast trot the one-ton workhorse bareback around the house several times. Today, when looking at the photo of us kids on Dick, I can't help but chuckle at the picturesque memory of Tim and his butt bouncing like a rag doll as Dick circled the farmhouse at a full trot. I envied Tim. If the tables were turned and I had been Tim, I would have been beaten with dad's razor strap, a reminder that the power of the razor strap hurt and emotionally affected me much more than a one-ton draft horse.

That spring, I received a gift from a class project. In school, we were able to watch chicks hatch and raise them, and when school closed for the summer, I was given one of the chicks.

My new friend and I went to Grandmas and Grandpa's in Vernonia, Oregon, for the summer. I was always elated to be with Grandma and Grandpa. No whippings for the whole summer, no teasing or being called dumb and retarded. I was given kisses and hugs. Grandma fussed over me and cooked nice things to eat, and I picked raspberries, and Grandma drowned them in cream. Grandpa had me help him in the garden, and it was my job to take care of the chickens.

My chick found its home in the chicken pen with Grandma's laying hens, where a brood hen adopted it. Early one morning, we awoke to a squeaky, crowing sound coming from the coop, and to my pleasant surprise, my pet chick had become a rooster. My rooster practiced his crowing just before sunrise each morning, and Grandpa thought it appropriate to name him Chatter Box.

That summer, Grandpa gave me a handcrafted bamboo fishing pole. He taught me how to catch crawfish, bait a fishhook with a crawfish tail, and catch native cutthroat trout. If only that glorious summer could have lasted forever.

3
Slugs Eat Dead Mice

We moved from the big house on Missouri Street to a smaller home on Lamphere Street in Southeast Portland.

My dad had stopped beating me. No razor strap intimidated me, and my stuttering had dissipated. I was ready for a fresh start—this year I was going to learn, sit at the front of the class, and be like everyone else. This was a new school, a new start, and things were getting better.

In 1953, I started the fourth grade at Baton Elementary School. My fourth-grade teacher was a pot-bellied man in his late thirties. He always wore the same brown sports coat with matching brown slacks. I wondered if he used the same rules that my mom enforced on me: wear the same school clothes all week, allowing for a change of shirts, wash them over the weekend, and then start over. He was friendly, laid back, and nonassertive. I do not recall his name, so I will refer to him as Mr. Brown.

Within a few weeks, it was apparent that I was a challenge Mr. Brown was not prepared for. Try as I may, I could not make any sense of the "foreign language" on the blackboard. Fractions, English grammar, searching for answers from a textbook—everything had moved up a notch, and in many ways, I was back at my second year in the first grade, trying to figure out "See Spot run" and simple addition problems. Every morning was like walking into a foreign country where nothing made sense.

Mr. Brown was kind and attempted to work with me one on one. However, as foreign as his teaching was to me, I was even more foreign to him. My progress was next to nothing, and I'm sure that he was as frustrated as I was. I found myself in the far corner of the classroom, for all practical purposes segregated from the rest of the class. I was out of sight and thus out of mind. I was left to gaze out the window and was rarely called on or asked to participate in class activities. I didn't exist!

My corner of the classroom became my special education corner, the window became my chalkboard, and nature was my teacher. I started by studying spiders. I saw spider webs among the rose bushes and shrubs outside the classroom window. By applying the same formula that I had used the past spring with the robins, I made mental notes about spider habits. When I got to my desk each morning, the web was heavy with silver droplets of dew. It amazed me that the web was strong enough to withstand the weight, though it sagged and bent. As the sun rose and the dew evaporated, the web returned to its former memory. *Wow, a spider web is strong,* I thought.

I observed how it could withstand the extremes of weather, such as wind and rain. One day, during recess, I purposely destroyed one of the anchor points of the web. As soon as I got back to my desk, I watched the web. Using the clock on the classroom wall, with its large black numbers and the dots between them (for hours and minutes), I figured out how long it took my spider to repair his web.

My window gave me endless opportunity to learn. Each day after lunch, seven crows appeared to clean up the playground, picking up scraps of bread, cookies, candies, and other discarded food. Chickadees followed them, and they spread out and swept the playground in military fashion.

During recess, I secluded myself at the corner of the playground and watched the other kids play. The boys chased the girls, and the girls were always able to outrun the boys but occasionally allowed themselves to be caught, a phenomenon I didn't understand.

One day, I found a dead mouse at the corner of the playground where nobody played. Normally, I would dispose of it by kicking it into the grass or picking it up by the tail and throwing it into the bushes. This time, I left it alone, and it became my next specimen to observe.

The next day at recess, I noticed a slug on the dead mouse. Mom had taught me that slugs and snails eat the bordering plants of the garden, and I had noticed them on Grandma's strawberries. The same type of slug that ate Grandma's strawberries was now eating a dead mouse. When I got home from school, I asked Mom, "Do slugs eat dead mice?" She said no, they only ate plant life. When I explained what I had witnessed on the playground, Mom shrugged her shoulders and went on with her business.

The next day, three slugs were eating on the mouse, and the day after that, only a slime spot and a tail were left. I was fascinated with what I had learned and wanted to share my new knowledge.

After class, I approached Mr. Brown and said slowly, so that I could be understood, that slugs eat dead mice. Mr. Brown told me that whoever told me that was mistaken, dismissed me, and continued with his paperwork. My shoulders dropped from the rejection as I left school.

After much pondering, I felt more optimistic. Nobody told me that slugs eat dead mice— I had learned it on my own, just like I had learned before how many worms a mother and father robin fed their chicks in an hour or how long it took a spider to repair its web, build a new one, or spin its victims in a cocoon to eat later on. The dead mouse experiment was a milestone. I thought, *Maybe I'm not retarded after all. I knew something that my teacher and mom didn't know! Wow!*

Encouraged by my discovery, I decided to take this experience a step further. When leaving class, I asked Mr. Brown if he knew how many worms robins feed their chicks in an hour. He said that he didn't.

"I do," I said.

"That's nice, Rodney." He ushered me out of the class and on my way.

Now there were two things I knew that my teacher didn't know. My special education class was working, and I was learning!

Toward the end of the school year, the teacher called on different students to verbally share points of interest that they had learned during the year. I felt I had something I could share and was elated when Mr. Brown called on me. I stood up and proudly asked the class as clearly as I could, "Do you know how long it takes a spider to repair its web or build a new one?" I should not have felt dejected by the laughter; after all, I was the forgotten "dumb" student who spoke funny and sat by the back corner window of the class, chewing his shirt collar.

When the class was dismissed, Mr. Brown pulled me aside and apologized for the class's reaction to my question. I took the opportunity to ask Mr. Brown if he knew the answer to my question. He apologized and said that he did not but that my question had no bearing on our curriculum for the school year.

I pondered as I walked home that day. School will be out in a few days, and there are a lot of things that I know that other people, including my teacher, don't! This is a good thing!

4

Grandpa

Shortly after fourth grade, my home life caved in. It was clear that my parents were divorcing, and I hated them for it. Years later in my reflections I wrote the two poems below to express my feelings.

Does my abyss have a bottom, for it seems so deep?
What pit is this that I have fallen into?
Darkness above me, darkness below me
engulfed in cold dark water above me and below me.
Which direction do I swim? For I have no pilot to guide me.

The divorce tore at me; I was confused and felt pressured to take sides. The brightness of learning in the corner of my classroom hid like a setting sun. Why the divorce? Why now, when everything was at last starting to come together for me? Why?!

So it becomes when one's spiritual fire
is covered by the physical motility of Earth.
Am I but four staffs swaying in a blissful breeze
of self learning to be thrown from my tower
that I worked so hard to build?

The summer after the divorce, Mom and my siblings moved in with my grandparents in Vernonia. I missed my dad! Even though I had been beaten to the point of missing school, I knew that my dad loved me, and there were good times to reflect on. This ability to identify the good in my dad helped me to overcome the blame, shame, and guilt of being the victim of his judgments.

Once we were settled at Grandma and Grandpa's, things went well for the summer. I spent most of my time fishing for catfish at the millpond and trout on the Nehalem River. Skinny-dipping at a secret swimming hole became a favorite pastime. I felt complete euphoria knowing that I was living with Grandma and Grandpa.

September meant another school year at yet another new school. I didn't even try to fit in or learn but portrayed myself as what everybody expected of me: retarded. I held firm to my First-Grade Life Agreement. It worked.

After my teacher reviewed my past school record, she allowed me to waste away at the back of the classroom. I maneuvered myself to a window seat and half-heartedly tried to start my special education program. However, my fifth-grade class was on the second floor and overlooked the eastern side of town. My view no longer consisted of spider webs and rose bushes but the main road through town and a residential area. All I had to entertain myself was an elderly lady who took her garbage out at the same time each morning. All I learned was that she always wore the same bathrobe, which left me to wonder if she ever washed it.

My grandparents, especially my grandpa, tried to work with me. I was given the book *Black Beauty*, but I struggled to get past the first sentence and quickly shelved it. Grandpa liked Al Capp's Li'l Abner comics and read them to me every Sunday morning. Al Capp's Joe Bfstplk became my favorite character. I looked at the pictures of this poor, wandering soul and related to him and his perpetual rain cloud "that followes him wherever's he go's."

I wanted to learn. I wanted to know why the sky was blue and not red like the sun. I wanted to know why the valleys were warm and the mountaintops cold. How did a radio pull words out of the air and put them into a box? Even more amazing, how did a TV work? On family outings along the Oregon coast, I stood on the shore, looking at the vast ocean, and wondered what was on the other side. My curiosity was exploding within my young soul. I wanted to know these things, but I struggled with finding the answers.

Around this time, while visiting the coast, I was watching for migrating whales with my Dad and Uncle Chuck when it came to me that the answer to my dilemma of learning lay with Simple Simon. "Simple Simon" needed a different environment. He needed an ocean, not a pail of water! I needed an ocean full of whales to learn from.

When my class was studying about the atmosphere, I raised my hand. The teacher called on me, and I asked hesitantly, in my broken speech, "Why is there snow on the mountains and not in the valleys, when the mountaintops are closer to the sun?" I was scolded for not paying attention to the subject being discussed. My question was never answered, and I did not ask questions again.

A week later while waiting for the school bus, I tried to crowd in front of my little brother, who was very proud of being in the first grade. Determined to defend his ground against all odds, he swung around, his lunch pail raised in his hand, to defend his territory. I stepped back to avoid the oncoming assault and ended up with my left foot under the tire of the approaching bus. I saw the tire slowly moving up my foot, onto my ankle, forcing my left leg flat, and all I could do was scream and pound on the fender. The bus stopped on top of my left foot and ankle. My brother and sister, along with the other kids, screamed directions to the bus driver who was panicked and trying to figure out where I was under his bus.

I looked toward the house. There was Grandpa running like a true athlete on a hundred-yard dash. He directed the bus driver off my foot and ankle, swooped me up in his arms, and carried me into the house. In 1954, Vernonia did not have a hospital or ambulance service. I found myself in the back of Grandpa's Desoto, speeding to Forest Grove some seventy miles away, where the nearest doctor was located. Soon I was wrapped up, on crutches, and headed back to Vernonia with damaged tendons and fractures.

I had to stay off my feet to allow my tendons to heal and hobbled around on crutches. The good news: no school! I confined myself to Grandpa's couch where I spent my days looking through Grandma's extensive collection of *National Geographic* magazines, Grandpa's farm journals, and my personal library of comic books. My grandma's friend, Mrs. Peach, visited and read to me from one of the *National Geographic* magazines lying on the table.

Mr. and Mrs. Peach lived down the road in a quaint, brown home with a freshly painted, white picket fence adorned with colorful flowers in accordance with the season. Upon entering her home, I caught the welcoming smell of fresh baked bread. She would cut off a thick, warm slice, cover it with blackberry or loganberry jam, and hand it to me along with a cold glass of milk.

What attracted me to Mrs. Peach was the way she taught. She taught Bible class stories using pictures and then read the same stories from the Bible. At first, when she started reading, I shied back in my chair, fearful of being called upon. She had a wonderful, perceptive spirit, and she never put me in an embarrassing situation by calling on me in front of the class. While telling Bible stories, she often gently rested her hand on my shoulder or tenderly stroked the back of my head and said something uplifting such as "You look like David with his slingshot" as she pointed to the picture of the lad David.

Mom continued to read to me from *The Child's World*. Grandma mostly read to me from *National Geographic*, and Grandpa read me the Sunday comics and from my comic books.

It wasn't long before I was off my crutches. After a boring day at school, at the closing bell, I anxiously got on the bus headed for home and my personal projects, which was perfecting my stalking ability and my figure-four traps to catch small game.

After the divorce, my dad temporarily moved in with his mother in Portland. It was weird to visit Dad in that environment. He didn't waste much time and was soon seeing another woman, which upset me very much. On the other end of the spectrum, my mom's new friend, Jack, was showing up on weekends to visit her. I absolutely hated seeing the affection that he showed my mother—it was a new experience seeing her receiving affection from a man other than my dad. It was difficult for me to process, and I reacted in the only way I knew and that was to shun Jack.

My Grandpa saw the pain and anger that I was experiencing. One spring day, while practicing with the bow that I received the previous Christmas, Grandpa approached and asked if I could hit an apple tree seventy-five feet away. With pride, I took aim and let the arrow fly. It flew straight and true to its mark on the apple tree. I received a pat on the shoulder and a "well done."

Grandpa and I found a grassy place along the river bank, and with the afternoon sun warming us, he talked about life. He explained that I would be knocked down many times in life and that I was not to allow that to stop me from obtaining what I wanted. He explained that my mother was going to marry Jack and there was nothing he or I could do about it, so I needed to prepare myself and learn to deal with it.

As we walked along the river bank, his arm around my shoulder, I said, "Bop, could you tell Grandma that I can swim so that she will let me go down to the river by myself to fish and look for frogs, crawdads, and periwinkles?"

Grandpa pulled me closer. "You know that your Grandma and I need to know that you can swim well enough to get to the river bank if you should fall in."

Careful not to reveal my secret skinny-dipping adventures, I said, "I am a good swimmer, Bop. I can swim across the pool in town. Just ask one of the Welch boys—they were there when I did it. I believe that if I fall into the river, I can swim well enough to get to the bank."

We were approaching a deep hole at the foot of some swift water. To my surprise, I felt Grandpa's strong hands grab me by the seat of my pants and the cuff of my neck. Before I knew what was happening, we ran toward the river, and I was in the air with nothing under me but the cold river. I went down like a rock, the cold water well over my head and stinging me like a million pinpoints. I struggled to the surface and clearly remember seeing Grandpa through the water, ready to rescue me if I needed him to. I broke the surface, gasping for breath, to find that I was floating down river in slower, deeper water.

Grandpa followed on the riverbank, yelling, "Swim, Rodney, swim hard, son! You can do this, I *know* you can do this!"

My boots felt like rocks on my feet, and my sweater felt like a lead vest, but I swam hard toward him. I kicked, clawed, chewed, bit, dug, and growled my way through the water and, exhausted, made it to the riverbank and into Grandpa's arms—looking like a whipped, cold, wet dog but alive.

Grandpa took my cheeks in his hands, looked me square in the eye, and said, "I believe in you, son, and I *knew* that you could make it to the river bank. It's a good start to believe in yourself, but to succeed, you have to have more than just a belief, you have to *know* that you can succeed. Now let's get to the house and Grandma to warm you up."

Upon arriving at the house, Grandpa marched into the living room where Grandma was sitting in her favorite chair, playing solitaire. Grandma was an immaculate housekeeper and never allowed anyone past the enclosed back porch with shoes or boots on, much less wet clothes. Nothing had been normal so far that day, so why would this be an exception?

"Pop, what in the world happened?" Grandma demanded as she came out of her chair.

"Mama, you don't have to worry any longer about this young man being down at the river alone. He can take care of himself just fine." Grandpa looked down at me, winked, and smiled. "I think he needs some hot chocolate."

Grandma was already on it, directing me to get out of my wet clothes as she tossed a towel to me to dry off, followed with a pat on the head and a smile that reminded me that I would always be her little boy, though to Grandpa I was growing into manhood. Years later, when revisiting the site of my swimming lesson, it didn't look that intimidating—if I had drifted a few more feet, I would have been in waist-deep water. As a boy, it was a scary experience, and to Grandpa, who knew his river, it was a life lesson.

That evening, while Grandma and Grandpa enjoyed their evening coffee, Grandpa invited me to sit beside him to listen to the radio. "Son (when he called me *son* at the beginning of a sentence, followed with a pause, it always meant that important instructions were about to follow), you seem to struggle at school. I know you're teased and not very well understood, and when you say you're dumb as some people think you are, that is not true. You have been given some challenges, and you are going to have to learn to deal with them. I have watched you, and you are not dumb. You have the same ability to see and figure situations out the same as anyone else in this world."

He continued, "Today, you took on a great challenge and overcame your fear by not panicking in the river. You pulled it together and got yourself out of what was a surprising and dangerous predicament." He took me by the shoulders, turned me so that I could hold his gaze, and said, "Life for you will be hard, and you will at times fall and at times fall hard." He lightly shook me. "Fight, son, and pick yourself back up! To try is to fail, to *know* is to succeed."

Grandpa was my hero, and I wanted to be like him in every way.

5
Blackbirds

As soon as school let out in June 1954, my mother married Jack, and we moved into a three-bedroom home on the outskirts of Roseburg, Oregon. I didn't like seeing my mom with another man. My mother didn't realize until after marrying Jack that he was an alcoholic; he was tolerable when sober, mean and cruel when drunk. I rebelled but not for long.

Jack set his standard, and he set it quick, firm, and without question. One evening when he had been drinking, I said something wrong, and before I knew it, horror entered my life. He grabbed me and threw me over the back of the living room couch. My face was forced sideways against the top back portion of the couch by Jack's strong forearm. He yelled at me not to move, saying he'd had enough of my disrespect and there would be no more. He left me there. Fear gripped my eleven-year-old body; I dared not even twitch. Jack returned with the upper half of a fiberglass fishing pole.

I would have welcomed a razor-strap whipping over the upper end of a fishing pole. When my father whipped me with a razor strap, I knew he still loved me, even though he had allowed himself to be a victim of passed-on behavior from his father. With Jack, it was as a master over his disrespectful slave.

The blows came hard from his strong arm, landing against my buttocks and legs. I screamed. It was days before I recovered from the welts and bruises. That day, I learned my place, and after that, I avoided Jack as much as possible, especially when he was drinking.

This was the first summer of living away from my grandparents. If ever there was a time I needed them, especially my grandpa, it was then. I went off into the nearby woods and looked north, wondering what it would take to find my way to Vernonia and my grandparents.

While walking through the woods with my air gun in hand, I once came upon a nest. I climbed up into the oak tree to examine it and found that it held four blackbird chicks. I was content to sit down and watch the nest to study the actions of the parents when they returned to feed their young.

I was angry at all there was. I lay in the grass, waiting to carry out a sinister plot that was forming in my mind. The feel of the air gun was warm and strangely friendly in my grip. The father blackbird returned to feed his young, and I felt jealous of the baby blackbirds, believing that they had more than me. I lifted up my air gun. The bead on my open sight was tight, resting at the base of the father's neck. I gave myself completely to fate and did not anticipate the shot; it had its own identity. I squeezed the trigger. PLUME—the father blackbird fell to earth.

I waited calmly for the mother, knowing that she would come. Not even her dead mate lying on the ground would stop a mother's instinct to feed her young. I waited until she landed on a nearby tree limb. I could have shot her dead right there if I wished, but I waited for her to land at her nest. On this day, my revenge, my fate, was fixed. There was no consciousness to my shot. PLUME—she fell dead beside her mate.

I climbed back up the tree to look at the chicks and began to realize the depth of my sinister deed. Four mouths opened wide. Four hungry chicks now had no parent to care for them. Mrs. Peach's teaching came back to me, "Not even a sparrow can fall to the ground and escape the knowledge of God."

I was overcome with guilt. How? From studying a nest of robin chicks, I knew that the blackbird chicks would starve quickly. I also knew that to protect themselves from predators, they would remain still in the nest until alerted by their incoming parents who, no thanks to me, were dead. There was only one thing to do. I carefully pulled the nest from its cradle of branches and took my adopted family home. A wrong had to be made right. My only fear was whether Jack would allow me to care for the chicks.

The chicks became a blessing in disguise. I learned that Jack had a tender side when it came to animals and saw him cry when he accidentally ran over our pet cat. He embraced the thought of my raising the chicks and talked my mom, also a meticulous housekeeper, into allowing them in my bedroom.

Within minutes, I was feeding them. Within an hour, I had organized my two sisters and brother into food

Image 4 Raising four baby blackbirds was a full time job of joyful penance.

gatherers. I gave each of them a can and sent them out to gather anything that crawled, buzzed, or hopped, as long as it fit down their throats.

I had to keep their food fresh and moist, as I realized early on that they depended on the fluid from whatever they ate to stay hydrated. By following the example of the other parenting birds, I carried the food, grubs, worms, and other little live things in my mouth, secured by my lower lip. It worked well.

When I wasn't feeding them, I was studying them. I observed other birds teaching their young how to fly and their first awkward attempts to flutter from limb to limb.

It was life or death for my chicks, and I was determined that life would be the winner! Their little wings began to coordinate with their bodies, and they soon experienced the glory of flight. Even after they learned how to fly, they were still learning to fend for themselves. At times, they dropped out of the sky to land on a nearby tree limb or other type of support, begging for a handout.

To this day, when we have a family gathering, my siblings often speak of the great effort we took to keep those chicks fed. The successful story of my blackbirds has been handed down to my children and grandchildren and will be passed on to my great-grandchildren.

The rest of the summer was uneventful, and when school was about to start, I had to take the name of my stepfather. I was to start the sixth grade not as Rodney Frank Williams but Rodney Frank Brosig. It was too much to handle.

I planned to run away and escape to the woods. I planned to separate myself from humanity and its cruelty. I had learned through the summer that by scavenging at the outdoor theater early in the mornings, I could find change on the ground. The nearby grocery center always had discarded produce in the garbage cans that was good to eat, and I wouldn't be noticed. Food, money—what else did I need? I had to act quickly. I stashed foodstuffs taken from the house and saved the money I found in the theater parking.

The weekend before school started, I got up early, grabbed some clothes and my money, jammed it all into a pillowcase, and climbed out my bedroom window.

I was eleven years old and heading into deep uncertainty. I climbed up the embankment behind my house and hid in the bushes where I had my stash of food items—not much but what I felt was a start. My perch allowed a view of the back of my home. As I looked down to where my family was still asleep, a strange feeling came over me. *I have control, for I'm hidden and can see you but you cannot see me. I can escape to the forests and hide, and from there I can see you but you will not see me.* This gave me the excuse I needed. This was power!

From my hiding place, I watched my mom walk through the house. I gave in to my fear and returned to my bedroom the way I had come out. Later in life, I realized that fear can be a good thing, and survival depends upon listening to that fear. I learned I must use fear correctly or I could never become the hero! I must at some time be the fool and take a blind step into my destiny.

I have no memory of sixth grade. All I knew was what I saw on my report card: straight Fs, except for P.E.

I fared no better in seventh grade. We moved again, this time to a white home on top of a hill in Winchester, Oregon. It was five miles north of Roseburg, overlooking the Umpqua River Dam. I was again required to enroll in junior high as Rodney Frank Brosig.

I was broken. I remember my little sister, Peggy, reading my comic books to me. My dog, Danny, died the year before, and Mom and Jack got me a dog that I named Rip after a dog in a book that Mom read to me. I rescued a wounded pigeon under the Umpqua River Bridge and had a paper route.

Seventh grade brought the same straight Fs except for P.E. I had no friends and no purpose to life. Thank God that life moves forward and the dark moments don't last. My future held light beyond what I could imagine, but more darkness was to come.

6
The Bullies

As soon as I was out of school, we moved again, this time to the small, agricultural town of Merrill, Oregon, just north of the California state line. We rented a ranch house halfway between the towns of Merrill and Malin.

The owner of the ranch, Felizberto Lorenz—or Old Portigo Joe, as he was known in the community—was a Portuguese immigrant from the Madera Islands. He lived in a shack behind the house with his ranch hand, Melvin Curlin. He ran a spread of Herefords or White-Face cattle, raised alfalfa and clover for feed, and maintained a productive apple orchard. Old Portigo Joe was an appreciative American and raised "Old Glory" on a flagpole in our front yard each morning.

Until this point, I had lived west of the Cascade Mountains, near the coast. This country was strange, with its open, arid landscape and the perpetual, sweet scents of sagebrush and juniper. For a kid who spent so much time by himself, it drew me into its serenity and became a sanctuary from the hard realities of life.

Shortly before school started, I narrowly averted a fight with three local bullies that I ran into behind a hot dog stand in Merrill. Rodriquez was the son of a ranch hand, Butch was the son of a local rancher, and Bruce was the son of the town mayor. I was the new kid in a small town. I backed out of the fight as bravely as I could, which was all the ammunition that this gang of three needed.

A week after this incident, I enrolled in class, still using my stepfather's name, Brosig. During lunch break, the gang of three stood behind the bleachers, wanting to fight me. They had attended school together since the first grade, and I was the first new kid. This was the opportunity that Rodriguez needed to step above his family's ranch-hand status and be better accepted by Butch and Bruce, not to mention the rest of the eighth-grade class. They circled me, taunting me.

I was the perfect target for them, because I saw myself as nothing more than the retard they treated me as. Rodriguez pushed me into the other two boys. I didn't fight back. They pushed and pulled me back and forth, then took turns hitting me on the arms and shoulders, one on each side. This went on until the five-minute bell rang.

Whenever the teacher left the room, they came over to my desk and took turns hitting me on the arms, all the time clucking like a chicken. They tripped me when walking down the hallway.

I was nicknamed "Brosig the Chicken" or "Cluck Cluck." They pretended to hand me an ice cream cone, and when I refused to accept it, they made me take it, then smashed it into my face and laughed, clucking like a chicken. They purposely dropped their books when no adults were around and told me to pick them up. When I reached down to do so, they pushed me over or kicked me, again clucking.

Before long, the seventh graders started bullying me, and then some of the freshmen boys. "Hey, Cluck Cluck, come here and pick up my books." I obediently complied, only to be kicked or pushed over.

I learned to survive like a wild animal by hiding or taking advantage of the areas where teachers gathered. I kept the bullying to myself; my mom and Jack did not know what was happening to me at school.

As summer turned to fall, my mother gave me a single-shot .22 rifle that had been given to her by her dad. She gave me two bullets, and I went into the sagebrush hills to hunt. I became an excellent shot. Cottontail rabbit, pheasant, and quail were soon supplementing our table, which made me feel like I was doing something good.

A dark cloud overshadowed me from the constant bullying at school, and it was spilling over at home with Jack. He had broken his leg on the job and was off work that fall. His drinking increased, and he was physically abusing my mom and me.

One day, after a light snowfall, I came across his footprints in the snow and found myself following his tracks and spitting in them. I was carrying a loaded gun and had a lot of built-up anger that needed a release—a bad combination.

About then, Mom gave me the news that Grandma and Grandpa were coming to visit and do some deer hunting. I was jubilant at first but then felt sad. I thought,

How could Grandpa like me, a coward lower than the chicken in the barnyard? At least a chicken would squawk and fly away if someone tried to kick it.

Grandma and Grandpa arrived on schedule. I was so glad to see them, and before long, I was off to the hills, hunting with Grandpa. Being with Grandpa did a lot to boost my self-esteem. We killed our quota of deer that fall, which helped with Jack being out of work. It made me feel good when I pulled my own weight to help the family.

My sister, Peggy, read to me from the comic strips in the daily newspaper. I was still in love with Li'l Abner, couldn't get enough of his adventures, and looked forward to being read to about him when school was out. I was bonded to the character with the perpetual dark rain cloud over his head. To me, Joe Btfsplk was the world's worst jinx, feared because nobody understood him and shunned because he looked and acted stupid.

I began to grow out of my speech impediment. I don't understand how this happened without therapy, but it did. Over the years, I had acquired a habit of running words together to camouflage my inability to properly pronounce them. Peggy was a natural nurturer, and she was always there to give me a helping hand, which included basic lessons in phonics with her fifth-grade level of understanding.

One night, Mom sat down with me and read the first chapter of the book *The Wahoo Bobcat* by Joseph Lippincott. That opening chapter captured me; I wanted the rest of the book, and I wanted it now. I didn't want to depend upon others to do my reading. It was time to read books on my own, and I was ready to do whatever it took.

I went to the bookshelf and pulled out volume one of *The Child's World*. It had been a long time since I had held the book, but when I opened it to the first page, it was like meeting a friend I hadn't seen for many years. There was the picture of a mother holding her baby and kissing him on the cheek. I remembered the words that my mother had read to me so many times: "Bye Baby Bunting, Daddy's gone a-hunting, to get a little rabbit skin, to wrap his Baby Bunting in."

I turned the page, and more old friends were there to greet me: the cow jumping over a smiling moon with a dish and a spoon running across a meadow, a cat playing a fiddle while sitting on a stone fence, a laughing dog. There they were, just as I had left them years ago: Old Hickory, Dickory Dock, Baa Baa Black Sheep, Mistress Mary, Quite Contrary, and This Little Pig Went to Market. There were thirty-six nursery rhymes, and I had memorized them all.

When the lights are out and everyone was asleep, I lit my bedside candle, opened my book of nursery rhymes, and then opened The Wahoo Bobcat. I put my finger on a word I'd memorized from the nursery rhyme and then searched for the same word in The Wahoo Bobcat. Sometimes I had to sound out the word in my head before matching them up. When this labor became too intensive, I started fanaticizing about the pictures, using a combination of images and the words I knew by heart. I became the shepherd boy with the Baa Baa Black Sheep, crooning with love for Mistress Mary.

Mistress Mary, quite contrary,
How does your garden grow?
With silver bells and cockle shells,
And pretty maids all in a row.

(Bjoland, 21)

I didn't understand the meaning of contrary and assumed that it was another word for beautiful, because I believed that Mistress Mary was beautiful. (Even after learning to read, whenever I came across the word contrary, I interpreted it as beautiful.)

I was beginning to wake up from a long, dark sleep that had lasted since the divorce of my parents, and I liked what I was waking up to. Through the rest of the school year, I put the memorized words from the nursery rhymes to the printed words in *The Wahoo Bobcat*.

One evening alone in my bedroom, I picked up *The Wahoo Bobcat*, opened it, and was lost with the first word at the top of the page, Preface. My heart dropped. I could not pronounce it, let alone understand what it meant.

I moved to the first sentence, "For years I followed his tracks," but could not read it well enough to understand it. I cried a deep, lonely cry. I had worked so hard to learn how to read, but I was what they said— simple, slow, retarded, a Simple Simon. As I had so many times before, I resigned myself to a fate of retardation. *The Wahoo Bobcat* lay on the floor, eventually to be lost.

I came home from school one day with a map of the states. We were to have a test and match the capitals to their respective states. My mom worked with me all week to memorize the state capitals, showing me where each state was on a map of the United States.

When the day came to take the test, I matched every capital with its state. The teacher kept me after class and said, "I don't know how you cheated to pass this exam, but I know you cheated."

I went home so angry that I was shaking and close to tears. My mom was livid but chose not to confront the teacher. My First-Grade Life Agreement was in effect, and my eighth-grade teacher was its enforcer. She had judged me according to my scholastic history. If only someone had understood that all I needed was some attention—some school administrator to look inside me and identify that spark that would become a flame—and work with my mother and me. It wasn't to be. No teacher could reverse my First-Grade Life Agreement: it had become law for all my educators.

My report card showed that I had to redo the eighth grade. I did not know what to do. No matter how hard I tried, there was no way to overcome the horrible curse that had been bestowed upon me.

We moved at the end of that summer to Klamath Falls and rented a home on the east end of town. I enrolled in the eighth grade for the second time at Klamath Central Junior High, a much bigger school. I had the routine down to a science and conducted myself like the good, semi-retarded boy.

When alone in the countryside, it was a different story. I often sat in the woods to watch the wildlife or people and think. On one occasion, while watching two coyotes play with a wounded mouse, I thought about all I had learned from building figure-four traps, tracking animals, and the family of robins. I thought of what I had learned from my window seat in the back of my fourth-grade class, raising blackbird chicks, and learning all the states and capitals.

As I watched the coyotes play with the mouse, I thought, I'm not dumb. People just think I am. Don't I know things that other people don't know? Am I the only person who knows that slugs eat dead mice? I came out of the woods determined to make a difference in school.

The opportunity came during my English class. One day at the close of class, the teacher handed out an assignment with words from a novel. We were to research and memorize the words, their meanings, and how to spell them, and we would be called on the next day to recite them from memory. I looked at the assignment, not understanding any of the words, but I thought, *I can do this, I know I can do this!*

I took my assignment home and sat down with Mom. I pointed to the longest word on the assignment and said, "Mom, will you teach me this word and how to spell it?" She got out the dictionary and began teaching me all that there was to know about the word, and by the time I went to bed, I had learned how to pronounce the longest word on the assignment page, its meaning, and how to spell it!

The next day in English class, I was excited and anxious to participate. I was *ready*! At the beginning of the class, the teacher asked if anyone wanted to volunteer. I stood up.

"I would," I said with gusto. The teacher looked at me with surprise, as did the rest of the class.

"Okay, Rodney." She raised her eyebrows in anticipation of what was to proceed from my mouth.

I looked her straight in the eye and said as clearly as I was able, "The word I choose to use is *philoprogenitiveness*, which means relating to or characterized by the love that parents have for their children. It is spelled p-h-i-l-o-p-r-o-g-e-n-i-t-i-v-e-n-e-s-s."

The teacher stared at me with disbelief. I heard gasps from other students, as if they were thinking, *How could Simple Simon do what he just did?* I was the only student who had mastered that word with its meaning and spelling.

After class, the teacher had me come to her desk. "Rodney, spell philoprogenitiveness."

I looked her in the eyes and spelled the word, without even a stutter, a second time.

"Rodney, you are unable to read correctly, and you cannot spell, so how did you do this? How did you take the most difficult word of the assignment and master it?"

"My mom taught me, and I learned it."

She said, "I would like to meet with your mother and learn how she taught you."

Wow, Mistress Mary, with her silver bells and cockleshells, I was riding high. I could give the meaning, pronunciation, and spelling of a word that few people could spell. My poor family! I started on Peggy, then my grandparents, and down the line to my cousins. Not one of them could spell philoprogenitiveness, but I *could*, and I did, a lot!

Within a week or so, we moved again, and my English teacher never met with my mom. Other than that eventful day, I remember little else of this time except Jack hitting Mom and then me when I came to her rescue. Jack introduced me to whiskey one Saturday night and got me drunk.

This time, we moved south of Klamath Falls to Ogden Street. Prior to enrolling in eighth grade for the third time, I begged Mom to allow me to use my birth name of Williams. To my surprise, I was allowed to. I was again officially Rodney Frank Williams. Even though I had built up resentment and a guarded fear of Jack when he was drunk, when sober, he surprised me with a genuine commitment to teach me how to defend myself. He showed me how to put my fists up in a defensive position to focus on the nose of the bully and deliver two left jabs followed with a right cross. It worked.

I was Joe Btfsplk, with my dark, raincloud following me wherever I went, and they could shun me if they wished, but they would not tease or bully me ever again.

Name B. rosig, Rodney Grade 8							
Nr. of Period	1st	2nd	3rd	4th	5th	6th	Result
Social Subjects							
Social Science	4	5	4-	4-	4-	4-	
Geography							
History							
English Subjects							
Reading	4	5	4-	4	4	5	
Language	4	8	4-	4-	4	5	
Spelling	5	5	5	5	4	5	
Skill Subjects							
Arithmetic	5	5	5	5	5	5	
Writing							
Appreciation Subjects							
Literature							
Art							
Music	4	3	3	3	3	3	
Physical Subjects							
Elementary Science	5	5	6	5	5	5	
Physical Education	2	2	2	2	2	3	
Health							
Industrial Subjects							
Manual Arts	4	4	4	4	4	5	
Home Making							
Days Present							
Days Absent	0	3½	4	3	6	6	
Times Tardy	0	0	0	0	0	0	

1	2	3	4	5
Superior	Above Average	Average	Below Average	Failing

CITIZENSHIP AND CHARACTER EDUCATION

The development of good citizens is the aim of the school. We desire the help of the parents so that each year may be one of learning and character growth for every boy and girl in our schools. Because of the importance of this type of education we are indicating here an estimate of the work habits and citizenship of your child.

	1st	2nd	3rd	4th	5th	6th
Work and Study Habits	4	4	4	4	4	4
Citizenship	4	4	3	3	3	3

Space for note, if desired:

Image 5 My first eighth grade report card.

7

Hoboin'

That fall, I was given a 16-gauge shotgun, and I was off to the hills hunting every chance I had. In 1957, it was not uncommon to see teenage boys with guns walking through the rural areas of Klamath Falls en route to and from their favorite hunting grounds—mine was the Hogback Mountain for rabbits and other small game. For ducks, I went to the slough areas on the east bank of Lake Ewauna along the railroad tracks on the west side of town. I especially liked this area because it gave me quick access to a variety of ducks, mostly mallards and pintails.

I was fourteen, and Mom had given strict instructions that while hunting along these railroad tracks, I was to avoid talking to anyone, especially the hoboes. To get to the sloughs and my favorite hunting spot, I had to go south of the Southern Pacific and Burlington Northern Railroad interchange. Near the interchange, there was a "hobo jungle" that was always occupied by at least a few hoboes. In passing, I was careful to give them a wide berth and not make eye contact, another defensive move that Jack had taught me.

My mother did not know that for me, the hoboes became a wonderful subculture of wandering, hard-working, homeless, downtrodden, shabbily dressed, on-the-fly freight hopping, jinxed souls, shunned by all the world, just like myself. It was destined that one frosty, fall morning while passing three hoboes sitting around a fire, one of them, a black man, called out, "Hey, boy." I was spooked and kept walking. Again he called with a deep, accented, voice, "Hey, Angelina boy."

I stopped and turned to give them my attention.

The hobo hollered, "Ya got any meat we can put in our banjo (a large cooking pot) boy?"

"No," I said nervously and started walking away.

"Angelina boy, we don't mean ta scare ya, but we need some meat for our stew." He pointed to the sloughs. "You shoot one o dem der coots out in da water, an we cook a good banjo stew for ya."

I mumbled, "Ya, ya, sure," and moved on.

One of the other hoboes called after me, "Good hunting, young man, and hope to see ya again."

The sound of the second hobo's voice calmed me, but I waved and moved on down to the sloughs.

Out in the water, I could see several black coot ducks swimming around the shallows. It would be an easy shot to get a few and to retrieve them. The more I thought about it, the better I felt about helping the hoboes out. I was well hidden in among the grasses. When I had a couple of coots lined up in my sights, a flock of about five pintails swooped in. Any duck hunter can tell you that when it comes to ducks, coots are at the bottom of the scale, so if you're going to give hoboes some meat, shoot the pintails. I waited, and two came within range. I drew down and took a bead on the two swimming close together. WHAM—the coots went skirting across the water, squawking, and the remaining pintails took flight, leaving two dead and drifting. I climbed onto a windfall that reached into the slough and waited for the pintails to come to me.

I could have stayed there, waiting for more ducks to return, and possibly get a couple more, or give these two pintails to the hoboes. *Why not? They don't seem dangerous, and Mom will never know*, I thought. With the pintails in hand, up the bank I went, headed to the hobo's camp.

I approached and was quickly put at ease with their warm welcome. In no time, they had the pintails cleaned, plucked, and in the "banjo" along with assorted vegetables. While the stew cooked, they invited me to eat with them.

This was my introduction to a class of people that I could understand and would bond with. I listened with wonderment to their stories of travel, work, and adventure. The hobo that had wished me "good hunting" was better educated than his companions and asked me where I was from and about my family and school. It was a wonderful few hours. Soon it was time for me to go home and the hoboes to go their separate ways.

Over the next few years, the hobos became a group of friends who understood and accepted me for who and what I was. I told Mom that I was camping while fishing, and that was exactly what I was doing except that I was also *flopping* (spending the night) with my new friends. Whenever I showed up at their camp, I brought an assortment of food. I snuck a small bag of beans from home, which they called *bullets*, and a rabbit, pheasant, or duck when I was hunting. Several of the hoboes called my wild game *gump*. It wasn't long before I was known and welcomed when "calling in" with hoboes I had never before met. I learned how to avoid the *Bull* (railroad security) and read the signs or codes for other hoboes posted at their jungles. I was given the handle "Hunter" because I brought wild game for the pot.

I knew the black hobo as Roadblock Jim or Jim—his *monica* (nickname) came from his stature—a good six foot six and broad shouldered. On a summer night, while flopping with several hoboes next to the interchange, Jim invited me to become a *road boy*.

"Hunter, you just plain blowed-in-the-glass good. I'm a thinken it a time fo you make a good road boy. I be catching a cannonball to Boise in da morn, you welcome to run with me yo want."

I heard a rich mix of laughter and chatter from the others.

"Now Hunter boy," one of the hoboes said, "you be careful of ole Roadblock, here. He be good glass that you can count on, but there be times he like to go steaming." Laughter followed.

Jim was quick to come back. "Yo Flap Jack, yo right, ya yo right, sometimes I do steamin it better then honey dippin o spearin your biscuits." They both laughed, and the others joined in.

Another hobo said, "Hunter, we havin fun here tonight and when we get done havin fun, we got some good angel food to eat, but you need to listen good, hear me?"

"Hu ya," I said, giving him my full attention.

"Flap Jack an Roadblock Jim, we all work for our grub, they no bums here. Our life, well, it's a hard, hard life, and at times we all have ta do some steamin an honey dippin."

Another hobo jumped in. "Honey dippin ain't so bad most the time. It pays good."

"That's cuz da boss, he can't find nobody but us to clean dem toilets," another said. "An all of us have ta spear dem biscuits. Hell man, you can find good junk an angel food from dem rich neighborhoods, spearin biscuits."

Jim stepped in. "I remember wheen ol' Flap Jack an I were on da Humboldt and we come across dis yegg (a hobo who steals from other hobos). I thak this bum, he was hot, an we all knows dis bum was a jungle buzzard grayback. Hells bells, just a few months befo dis yegg had turned Flap Jack's pockets while he was on da rum. Well, my good ol friend here he jus up an rum-dummed dis yegg real good, den turned da pockets oh dis bum for some snipes an a couple o nickel notes and then flipped him south ta Reno."

I learned that *angel food* was a chocolate cake that one of the hoboes had found while *spearing* a dumpster behind a grocery store.

This was my second year, my third residence, and my third school to complete the eighth grade. I was a lost cause. I saw no sense in attending school. I skipped school and spent my days on Hogback Mountain, honing my survival skills and watching people.

I found a high ground near a residential area and watched people with binoculars. It was like being "outside the box" while everyone else was "inside," an ability that would become an asset in my future employment. I thought that it was only a matter of time before I was caught and in trouble, but it didn't happen. Nobody seemed to care—not my parents and definitely not the school.

My second year in the eighth grade came to an end, and I flunked again, as expected.

No one asked, "How long do school administrators recommend that a student keep repeating a grade?" I guess the answer was simple: Advance the student to high school under a conditional status, and allow the system to work. He will get the picture, drop out, and become the ditch-digger or by some miracle overcome the odds stacked against him.

Tildsley suggested that, "It is a frank recognition by an educator that all men are not created equal, at least that they are not equal in the elementary stage in their capacity for book learning" (Tildsley). Sadly, this thinking had influenced the education system of the 1950s. The teachers who felt a need to bring special education to the front, to help students as myself, were few and for the most part not heard. Parents from the lower-income side of life, like mine, left schooling to the teachers, and the teachers believed that they knew about educating children better than the parent. Students like me slipped in that vast canyon of misunderstanding between teachers and parents.

I spent most of that summer with my grandparents where I received a reprieve from Jack and his drunken abuse. Deep inside, I knew that I was not going to make it in society. I could ask to live with my grandparents, but why? I was going nowhere. I would be a disappointment to the two people I loved the most.

SUBJECTS	FIRST SEMESTER									SECOND SEMESTER									
	First G	C	Second G	C	Third G	C	Exam.	Average G	C	Fourth G	C	Fifth G	C	Sixth G	C	Exam.	Average G	C
Math								4	2	4	2	4	2				4	2
English								4	2	5	2	5	2	4	3		5	2
Spelling								5	2	5		5	2	4	2		5	2
Phys. Ed.								4	3			3	3	2	2		3	3
Science								3	3			4	2	5	2		4	2
Art								5	2			3	3				3	3
Shop										3	2	3	3				3	
Soc Studies / Times Tardy												5	2	5	3	5	5	3
Music / Days Present												2	2	2	2		2	2

EXPLANATION: Citizenship—In arriving at the grade for Citizenship the following habits and traits were taken into consideration: Carefulness, cooperation, courtesy, dependability, initiative, fairness and industry. Citizenship grade is given in column marked "C."
Grade Marks: 1, 94-100; 2, 86-93; 3, 78-85; 4, 70-77; 5, failure; Inc., incomplete; W, withdrawn.

Image 6 My second year in the eighth grade - I managed to get tolerable marks in Art, music and PE - all other classes it was 4's and 5's (today's equivalent of D's and F's)

8
Eighth Grade Forever

What is this faint spark deep within my soul that refuses to die? Where is the source that feeds it, however so slightly? I know not, but I am grateful.

I started my freshman year at Henley High School. For the first time since the third grade, I was living in the same home as the year before. It felt good to start school with familiar faces.

I had never played football other than some touch or flag football in a cow pasture. I was invited by the high school football coach to turn out for practice, and this was a real boost to my self-esteem. I became an instant success on the football field and earned the positions of left defensive end and alternate left tackle.

I had played a few games when the coach pulled me aside after practice and told me that my grades were too low. I could show up for practice but could not suit up and play in the games until I pulled my grades up. I knew that wasn't going to happen but continued to show up for practice to prove myself before my peers. For the first time, I was looked at as something other than a retard.

Later in the season, I was approached again by my coach, and he asked me if I had a girlfriend. When I said no, he suggested that I "land a girlfriend" and have her tutor me. I was taken aback and didn't know how to react—I had never given any thought to having a girlfriend. Who would want to go out with Simple Simon, a dumb retard?

As destiny had it, a family moved in across the street, and they had a beautiful daughter named Sue. Whenever I was within twenty feet of her, my stomach turned over, but I finally worked up the courage to talk to her. She didn't reject me. I got up the nerve to do the impossible, ask her out to the movies, and she accepted. Success!

She informed me that I would have to ask her dad for permission to take her out. You had to be kidding me! He was a big Irishman. Silver bells and cockle shells, this man didn't smoke the cigars he carried in his mouth all the time, he ate them! Little dumb me asking him for permission to take his daughter to the movies?

I looked at this beautiful, petite, Irish lassie with her cute, crooked smile and was captured, a fish on a hook to be reeled into those enchanting blue eyes. "Huh, okay," I said.

I had no idea how I was going to accomplish the task, but there was no stream swift enough, no ocean wide enough, no mountain high enough to stop me, not even a six-foot-six-inch, 250-pound, cigar-eating, construction-working dad. I was determined to take Sue Kennon to the movies.

I spent the next two weeks working up the courage. I stood in front of the bathroom mirror and practiced with the most manly, macho voice I could muster. I practiced using a formal approach and then changed to a more conventional approach. Mom came to my rescue and told me to just be myself and keep it simple. I figured that the worst that could happen was him saying no.

My plan was to catch Mr. Kennon when he came home from work and approach him in his driveway as he got out of his car. The day finally came. With as much bravado as I could muster, I approached him to make my request. I stood there looking up at this big Irishman with a stub of a cigar clapped between his teeth, and finally made my first brave, squeaky, stuttered attempt.

"Mis-ss-ter Ke-ke-ne-ne-on?"

This isn't working very well, I thought. My next approach was performed with a deeper voice, but the stuttering was still present.

In the end, he invited me to come inside and talk on the living room couch. "I understand that you wish to take my daughter to the movies."

"Yes, sir," I said, being careful to speak clearly and not in the hobo slang that I had acquired.

He gave me permission to take his daughter to the movies and instilled in me something that I now use with my own daughters. He explained how much his daughter meant to him, how she was his princess and he was her knight in shining armor, and he told me that I was to treat her as the princess she was.

The date went well—Mom taught me the etiquette of opening the car door and other important things pertaining to a first date—and I now had a girlfriend. Yes sir, I was King of the Mountain. I was somebody, because I was dating without question the prettiest girl in the school.

I did not ask Sue for help to get my grades up, because what I needed was a miracle. I needed the Grim Reaper to kill my First-Grade Life Agreement and destroy prejudgment. Though my football coach did not contribute to my Life Agreement, it still dominated my environment.

Football season ended, and wrestling season was starting. I came from a family of wrestlers, and Jack had wrestled in high school. I had friends. I had a girlfriend. I had purpose.

I had to get something other than failing grades on my report card. I had to find help, and once more I found that in my sister. My seventh-grade sister was a champ. She was able to get me through enough of my homework (along with some cheating on my part, albeit with some guilt) to enable me to squeak by with the required grade.

I made the wrestling team and quickly rose to the top of my weight class. I was winning. On school days, I wrestled, and on weekends, I boxed at the YMCA. I was becoming a grappler. I knew how to take a man down and how to hit. I was undefeated in boxing and in wrestling until I got to state regional playoffs in wrestling and lost to a senior. I was a winner and lettered in wrestling, which meant that I was not only equal but superior in something recognized by the administrators of my First-Grade Life Agreement.

One day while Peggy was reading to me, she stopped at the word *thinking*. She put her thumbnail between the *k* and the *i* and explained what a syllable was and how to pronounce words by recognizing syllables. I thought, *Like Mom did with me in learning phi-lo-pro-gen-i-tive-ness.* I retrieved *The Child's World* and went to work reading and rereading my memorized nursery rhymes.

At school, I paid attention to class and gave it my very best. I remember thinking that if only I could at least learn to spell *school* correctly, I would be on my way, but things didn't come to me the way that they did to others. I saw things differently than anyone else.

Mr. Bullock taught English, and I took a keen interest in his class, knowing that I needed to better understand English if I was to make it in this world. One day in class, Mr. Bullock described the intricate detailed use of the colon and semicolon. I wasn't anywhere close to finding any rhyme or reason behind what he was trying to get across to me. Although I knew he was talking about some form of punctuation, in my simple, logical manner of processing, I had a completely different picture in my head. I knew from the teachings of my mother and grandmother that you eat greens and salads "to keep your *colon* clean." Your colon was the waste disposal passage of your body, and why would you name two dots after your colon? Mr. Bullock went on to describe a semicolon. I knew what a *semi* was; my dad and Jack

67

were diesel mechanics and worked on semi-trucks and tractors. I pictured a great big semi-truck going full bore down my colon, pushing a load of poop into the toilet to be flushed down the sewer. Whatever Mr. Bullock had tried to convey to me about punctuation was completely lost, and I knew I was too far behind to ever catch up with my class.

To compensate, I began to cheat, but even cheating didn't result in a sustained passing grade. Cheating made me feel dirty and low, and in the end, I decided that I would rather fail than cheat. My cheating was like the ancient mariner's albatross, and it hung heavily around my neck.

> "And I had done an hellish thing,
> And it would work'em woe:
> For all averr'd I had kill'd the bird
> That made the breeze to blow.
> Ah wretch! Said they, the bird to slay,
> That made the breeze to blow!
>
> Ah! Well a-day! What evil looks
> Had I from old and young!
> Instead of the cross, the Albatross
> About my neck was hung."
> (Coleridge)

I quit cheating, and it wasn't long before I was out of sports. My self-esteem dropped. I no longer felt worthy of Sue, drifted away from her, and went back to my safe place of being outside "the box" looking in.

My freshman year came to an end. I had successfully lettered in wrestling, but to accomplish that, I reverted to what I had committed not to do: cheat.

The following summer, I went to work for Klamath Ready Mix. I chipped cement that had set up in the trucks mixing hold for fifty cents an hour. After work, I was boxing at the YMCA, and my weekends were mostly spent fishing and "jungling up" with my hobo friends at the railroad interchange. I had learned to function outside the box; I was confident in my ability to take care of myself and had a plan to escape from society. I would disappear. The thought was intriguing, and imagining the self-confidence to follow through with it gave me a sense of worth.

During my adolescent years of the 1940s and 1950s, society had abandoned me to the wilderness of self-preservation. I had not adequately learned to pronounce or write English, nor had I learned the rules of grammar other than what little my sister gave me.

I lived in a self-imposed solitude and later related this state to the confused, disillusioned Philip Nolan, who stated during his court martial, "Damn the United States! I wish I may never hear of the United States again!" (Hale). Nolan was sentenced to never hear the name of the United States again. He was set out to sea, never again to set foot on his country's soil, and became known as The Man without a Country.

Unlike Nolan, I was welcome to leave my confinement, re-enter "the box," and participate in society, but I felt that society didn't want me, and I didn't want society. There were times when I felt a panicky need to escape. Occasionally I ran into the woods and crawled deep within the brush, under a windfall or some other closed-in hiding place. I curled up and waited for the feeling to pass. When it did, I went to the edge of the woods and watched people, thinking, *I can see you, you cannot see me.* In my freshman year, I learned how to project myself into and out of "the box" as I wished, but I did not realize that I was slowly retarding, becoming more feral than human in my thought process.

During the summer of 1959, I was asked to participate in a large boxing match, sponsored by the YMCA and the Klamath Indian Reservation. It was held in Chiloquin, Oregon, north of Klamath Falls. The weekend of the event, Jack took me there along with a couple of other team members. This was going to be a big event: news coverage, cameras, and boxing scouts, the whole shebang. We were going up against the U.S. Air Force boxing team based at Kingsley Field. Right away, I knew that we were in trouble. We looked like a team of ragamuffins from the wrong side of town, using discarded equipment from our robes to our gloves, while the Air Force opponents had the best equipment that money could buy. We were intimidated by the Air Force, I more than the others, because I was to be the main attraction. I had been matched with their black belt martial arts instructor.

When the smoker (boxing match) started, we started getting our asses kicked right away. We were losing every match, and the closer we got to the final match, the more nervous I felt. Finally, it was my bout. I climbed into the ring, went to my corner, and sat down to look across the ring at this mean-looking guy, rolling his gloves together, staring across the ring at me. I was spooked. All I could think of was that he was an Air Force martial arts instructor. Why was I matched with this giant? I was shaking so badly that my coach had to hold me down on my bench. He gave me the usual words of encouragement that went straight over my head and out the ventilation vents along with the odor of sweat and blood. I looked down at the spit bucket, which had yet to be emptied from the previous bout, and all I saw was blood and mucus.

The bell rang, we met in the middle of the ring, touched gloves, and my opponent started in on me. It was obvious that he wanted to knock me out in the first round. I covered up and started backpedaling around the ring. That's pretty much how the rest of the round went, me backpedaling while covering up from the wild punches that didn't land anywhere that would hurt me. At the end of the first round, my coach was upset.

"Williams, you lost that round to a guy that doesn't know how to box. You are a boxer, he's not, now box and knock this bum out!"

"I'll try, Coach," I said as the mouthpiece was put back into my mouth.

My coach put both hands on my face, squeezed, looked into my eyes, and scolded me. "I didn't set this match up for you to *try* to win. I matched you up with this guy to win! Now go out there, box, and take care of business!" My coach was right. I knocked my opponent out in the third round.

September was upon me, which meant my sophomore year. I had received some excellent reviews from my fight and was scheduled to fight in another event in October. This was going to be a better match. I was to fight a guy from Medford, Oregon, called The Fighting Irishman. I liked the name; I was Irish with an inherited Welsh name, so why not? If I beat this guy, I could take his nickname. I liked the sound of it.

My high was temporary. As soon as school started, I found myself attending the ninth-grade classes that I had failed the year before. Sports were out—I wasn't able to read well enough to understand the textbooks or exams, and I was convinced that there was nothing left to do but quit school. I set a departure date for April. I had a lot to keep me busy, and skipping school became a regular occurrence.

On the south slope of what the locals referred to as Hogback Mountain, I found the perfect location for a cache. It was dry and well protected by an outcropping of boulders. I cached canned foods, wool and cotton clothing, rain gear, and quarter-inch hemp line. These would allow me to be the hermit I planned to become.

This was not a lonely time, because I rejoiced in escape. I withdrew to my mountaintop of complete solitude to avoid people. Years later, I wrote the following poem about my experience.

My solitude is the silence of the tide
pounding upon the rocks with its foam
spewing up to be caught in the wind.

My solitude is the silence of a
woodpecker pounding a tune on a
hollow cedar.

My solitude is the silence of a raccoon's
chatter scolding me for not leaving a
scrap from my dinner.

My solitude is the silence of a sea
breeze rustling the forest trees as it
carries the evening fog.

Why is this my solitude?

Because I am the only ONE to hear it.

9
First Passed Test

I was at my friend's home when the phone rang, and I heard my sister, Peggy, crying, "Rodney, they're fighting." Jack was drunk and had hit Mom and my little sister, Linda. I hung up and ran home as fast as I could.

Enough is enough! No more!

I came through the front door to see Jack next to the fireplace in a drunken stupor. He ordered me to get an armload of firewood off the porch. I looked toward Mom and saw Linda, who was nine years old at the time, sitting next to Mom on the couch; the left side of her face was flushed from being struck.

I didn't pick up an armload of wood but selected a two-foot long piece of wood and entered the house. Jack knelt in front of the fireplace, his back to me, and I focused on the back of his head, thinking, *I know that I can do this. One tremendous blow, and we won't have to put up with you and your abuse anymore!* I needed to move quickly before he turned around.

Just as I was about to swing the wood and secure the well-being of my mom and siblings, I glanced at Mom and saw horrified fear on her face. She looked me in the eye and silently shook her head to say NO! I was caught by the powerful grip of her stare, and I knew that if Jack turned and noticed me, there would be a horrible fight. I had a split second to retreat or do what I felt must be done.

I turned and went back out on the porch to get the armload of firewood.

Within an hour, Jack was passed out on the bed, snoring. I pleaded with Mom to divorce Jack, but she made no commitment.

The next morning, as Jack lolled in bed with a hangover, I confronted him, and he said that he was sorry for what had happened the evening before. He had never apologized to me before. I saw the remorse in his eyes and wondered, *Is there any hope for this bum? Is he able to stop drinking and abusing our family?* Fully expecting to be backhanded, I mustered my courage and told him that if he ever laid a hand on my mother or siblings again, I would beat him to a pulp with a baseball bat when he was asleep. Jack was capable of breaking me in half, which I was expecting to happen at any second, but he stared at me with a sad look and said nothing.

After Thanksgiving, my mom was at a loss on what to do. I was sixteen and about to drop out of school. Jack was drunk most of the time, and I was determined not to allow him to continue his abuse. Mom came up with a plan; she approached me and asked if I would like to see Japan. My heart spoke to me with a clarity stronger than any rational thoughts. I understood and said, "Yes." I was back in the box.

The next day, I closed my locker door and walked out of school, never to return. I said nothing to the teachers or anyone in the office, not even my friends. *Out of sight, out of mind. Simple Simon the retard is gone, and we don't have to deal with him anymore.*

On December 18, 1959, the day before my seventeenth birthday, Mom took me to meet with a Navy recruiter. She signed a waiver that allowed me to be recruited.

The recruiter escorted me into a room, explaining that I needed to take a generic, multiple-choice entrance exam. Pure fear enveloped me, and I flunked. The recruiter said that it was most likely due to nerves and gave me a textbook to study. He told me that the questions and answers were in the book and to come back in two weeks to retake the test.

I went home, opened the book to find that it looked like all the other textbooks—full of words that did not match my nursery rhymes. I struggled to pronounce them, let alone know what they meant, but I was on my own. Mom was too emotionally involved in dealing with Jack to come to my aid.

Mom took me to the Navy recruiter again, and I took the exam and flunked it again. The recruiter mentioned the possibility of a conditional waiver because of a conflict starting in an Asian country called Laos. He said that he would look into it and get back with us. Mom didn't wait. The next day, I was on a Greyhound bus headed north to Grandma and Grandpa's. If I had stayed,

I knew that something horrible would happen between Jack and me, and I believe that Mom knew it too.

Once settled in with my grandparents, I was connected with the local Navy recruiter to take the exam a third time. I flunked it and was given the same textbook, but this time Grandpa, in his wisdom and straightforward way, came to my rescue.

Grandpa and Grandma took turns reading the questions in the book to me, pointing at each word and requiring me to repeat after them word for word. On and on, pointing out each answer, making me repeat each one, again and again—would they ever stop? I feared not.

The big day was approaching, and it was my last chance to pass. I was torn between the desire to retreat to a mountain lair or to make my grandparents proud and somehow pass that exam. Living with my grandparents was always different from living at home; with them, I felt no urge to escape. I was loved and respected, I received one-on-one attention, and I was given responsibilities with direction and praise. I wanted to please the people who loved and believed in me.

I went into the exam room along with several other recruits and took the dreaded test. I recognized several of the questions from going over them repeatedly with my grandparents and hoped that I had gotten the answers correct, but for the most part, I was guessing.

When the test was over, I was called into a separate office, as I had been after the previous exams. I sat down across from the man who issued the test and knew what was coming. I thought, *I've given this my best shot; there is nothing more I could have done.* He smiled and informed me that I had passed by one question. Hot dang, heaven be blessed with Little Boy Blue come blow your horn—I passed that test!

I joined the other recruits, and we were all taken to a hotel to spend the night. The next day, I said goodbye to my grandparents and was on an airplane with the other new recruits headed to boot camp in San Diego, California. Once we landed, we were put on a bus headed for the U.S. Naval Recruiting Base of Camp Nimitz. When we stepped off the bus, we were met by a big, broad-shouldered, square-jawed, red-headed Chief Boatswain Mate. He stood with shoulders squared, hands clasped behind his back, and feet exactly ten inches apart, tall and straight to greet us. "Listen and listen well, for I will give you a command once and only once." I knew then that my life was about to change.

The physical part of boot camp was uneventful, but the academic part was a nightmare. I passed a few written exams only because I cheated. I was well aware that I was only cheating myself.

The hands-on exams were a different story, and I aced them. I thought, *Maybe all this will balance out, and I can do this without cheating on the written exams.* I scored the highest in my unit on the firing range. I could tie any seaman knot that was thrown at me, and during knot-tying contests, I could tie a bowline, blindfolded, within one second. I could partly untwist and then interweave a hemp or manila line (rope) to make a long, short, and back splice, and in the same manner splice an eye at the end of a line, all faster than any of my mates. I could swab a deck quicker and cleaner than any other boot sailor. The spit shine on my shoes couldn't be matched. I could make the big brass bell at headquarters shine like a mirror so that the Admiral himself could shave with it.

I could do all that but could not pass a single written exam. This and buying into the belief that I was a slow learner was starting to irk me. This First-Grade Agreement smacked me at every turn.

At the end of boot camp, we had one final exam, and we were told that it was a review of everything we had covered during our fourteen weeks. We had to pass it to graduate and move on to our assigned duty stations.

The big day came with several units assigned to take the exam. I looked at the exam and figured that the odds were with me, and why shouldn't they be? Humpty Dumpty could fall off that wall only so many times. We were told that the test would be multiple choice. I had a one in four chance of guessing right, and after flunking so many multiple-choice exams, this had to be my lucky day.

A few days later, I was called into the instructor's office and told that I had failed. He told me they were going to give me a second chance, and if I didn't pass it, I would be given a discharge from the Navy. I was in deep trouble and knew it.

I called my grandpa.

"Bop, I failed my final exam. I just can't grasp what they want me to understand."

"You don't understand, son, because you can't read, am I right?"

"Yeah, I guess so. Bop, I don't know enough of the words on the paper to understand."

Not one to mess around with words and not afraid of the more colorful ones, Grandpa let loose. "Don't you dare give up on this! Your balls are to the wall, son, so get your ass in gear and pass that test. Are you listening to me here, son?"

"Yes, I hear ya, Bop."

"Good. Go find some place where you can be alone and say your prayers, because you're going to need some help from the ol' man upstairs. I want you to listen closely to what I going to say. Be honest, son. Tell whoever is going to give you this test the truth, that you can't read well enough to understand the questions. Let things just happen as they may. Maybe they can make some other kind of arrangements. If not, you know you have a home to come back to."

"Okay, Bop, I'll try."

Grandpa sounded like my boxing coach. "No, son, don't try, just *do it*! Walk in there like you own the damn place! Be confident and take care of business."

"Okay, Bop, I'll do it!"

I hung up the phone, wanting to believe that I could do it.

I still had a deep desire to escape to be free. I wanted to disappear from society, and all I had to do was walk off the base, put on my civvies (civilian clothes), go to the train yard, and catch a Cannonball or Hot Shot to

Klamath Falls. I hoped that no one had stumbled onto my cache and that it was still in good shape on Hogback Mountain.

I had to pass the exam if I expected to graduate and continue on in the Navy. Two days before my exam, I went before my instructor and made a full confession, telling him that I could not read well enough to understand the exam, and even if it was read to me, I would not be able to express my answer in writing. I said, "Sir, only my little sister can understand my scribbling—that is truthfully what it is—and she is in the eighth grade." My instructor, a first class petty officer, asked several questions about why I couldn't read or write and how I had passed the entrance exam for the Navy. He said that he would see me in a few days when I was scheduled to take the test.

I showed up on schedule, walked in, and found that I was the only one there to take the test. I was instructed to take my place at a fold-up table, and my instructor and a lieutenant junior grade sat on the opposite side.

The lieutenant asked me a lot of questions similar to those I had been asked before. He asked me to verbally recite the alphabet, and I did. He asked if I knew multiplication, and I said I didn't except for what I could do on my hands, so I was restricted to twos, fives, and tens. He told me that I would still have to take the same test as before and there would be no exceptions, but he wanted to personally administer a separate, verbal test. He would ask a question, and I would have to write the answer as best I could. I took the pencil and a tablet of paper and waited.

The lieutenant said, "Write the following words vertically down the page. There, as in *over there*."

Wow, this is a simple one to start with, I thought. I know how to spell *air* and I knew that there was a *th* in the word, so I wrote *thair* and looked up for the next word.

"Absent." I wrote *apsens*.

"Soldier." I wrote *sowjer*.

"Marine." I wrote *murren*.

"Sailor." I wrote *sylor*.

"Shoulder."

I knew I was in trouble, because I pronounced *soldier* and *shoulder* the same. I gave it my best shot and wrote *sowger*. I was confident that I would get a least one word correct.

The Lieutenant had me write a few sentences, and I handed him my paper and waited.

A smile moved across his face. "I believe you," he said, looking at me over the top of my paper.

"Sir?"

"I believe you when you told your instructor that only your sister can read or understand your writing."

"I'm sorry, Sir," I said, confused.

The Lieutenant explained that the exam would be administered verbally. My instructor would read the question to me, followed by the multiple-choice answers. I was to give an answer verbally, and my instructor would mark my answer on my test paper.

I got a break, but the instructor was not that patient with me. He read the question along with the multiple-choice responses, and I asked him to repeat them a few times. He reluctantly accommodated me, but for the most part, it was a one-shot deal. When we were finished, he excused me, and I went back to my barracks.

I was called in the next day and told that I had passed. I was promoted from a recruit to an apprentice seaman and was to stand by for my orders of deployment. For the first time in my life, I felt a sense of pride and accomplishment. I had made it! The Navy did not write me off as retarded and had given me a chance to use my auditory learning skills to advance, unlike previous administrators and teachers.

Within three days, I received my orders along with two weeks' leave. I was assigned to the USS Lincoln County Landing Ship Tank (LST) 898 out of Long Beach, California.

10
Navy

I had two weeks' leave before I had to report for duty. Once home in Klamath Falls, I caught a Greyhound bus to Vernonia to visit my family. Mom, Grandma, and Grandpa were proud and seemed relieved that I had made it through boot camp and into a structured environment.

The emotions of being home, if only for two weeks, made me question the reality of my future. Could I really survive any better with my peers in the Navy than I had with the kids in school? My fears were magnified because of my inferiority complex and being deemed less intelligent than my peers. I was able to work hard and perform well when assigned a physical, hands-on assignment, but I was haunted by the fear that I would be handed some written form of communication and expected to understand it or, worse yet, given a written assignment. I had been through this in school—why would being in the Navy make any difference? Could I adapt to a structured society with its rules and the perpetual fear of being embarrassed because of illiteracy? How long would it take before Simple Simon appeared?

The natural reaction of a terrified child or adult is to retreat to a secure environment and curl up in a fetal position. I wanted to find a safe place and wish all fears away, to feel the softness of my mother and hear again her sing, "Bye Baby Bunting, Daddy's gone a-hunting, to get a little rabbit skin, to wrap his Baby Bunting in…"

I seriously thought about running away, separating myself from society, becoming a truly feral man. Back in Klamath Falls, with time on my hands, I decided to "jungle-up" at the railroad interchange. I thought that hoboing would be a good way to satisfy the deep, constant desire to escape from "the box." Entering the Navy was putting myself *in* the box with no way out.

One night, I met a couple of Depression-era hoboes and got some good advice: stay in the Navy. I had to look at it in proper perspective. Catching my ship was like catching a good train. The hoboes said, "Enjoy your ride. You're gettin three squares a day and a free ride around the world. Besides, you go desertin, you will be duckin the law the rest of your life. You're hooked, Hunter, so you gotta deal with it."

It was time to face reality. I was bound to the Navy.

As scared as I was, I packed my bag and headed out. Mom dropped me off at the Greyhound depot to catch my ride to Long Beach, and my first duty station. When I got out of the car, kissed Mom goodbye, and walked into the depot, a sick feeling hit me in the stomach. I was going into an environment that I had no control over and no escape from. Would I be able to adapt?

I sat in the bus station, listening to the background noise of a radio news report about Castro and Cuba. I was ready to head up to the Hogback and my cache and out of society. Just when I was ready to run off, who appears out of nowhere, with his bindle (personal belongings) and all—the same hobo who advised me at the jungle.

"I'm thinkin of doggin it down to Stockton. I hear they got plenty o' work down that-a-way. Mind if I ride with ya?"

I moved my sea bag to make room.

"You're kinda nervous, ain't ya?"

"Yeah, kinda."

"We hobos have a saying, and that is if ya want to ride the rail alone, never let anyone know where and when ya gonna jump the train. Sometimes we like or need some company. I'm a-feelin you could use some company, so I decided to jump a ride with ya and dog it to Stockton."

We talked until the call came to load up, sat together on the bus, and visited through the night. I got some sound survival advice. He told me if after I got out of the service, if I wanted to go hoboing, I should leave a mark at the Klamath Falls jungle, and we would hook up. I knew that he could have saved the cost of a ticket and ridden the rail to Stockton, but he was actually there for me, and now that we were dogging it, I was glad of it.

While he was sleeping, I took a five-dollar bill out of my wallet and stuck it in the pack of cigarettes in his coat pocket.

We pulled into Stockton in the predawn hours, said our goodbyes, and as the bus was pulling out, I watched the hobo, with his bindle over his shoulder, stand alone under a streetlight and pull out his cigarettes. He saw the bill, looked up at me, and smiled. We waved at each other. He gave me a thumbs up and walked away, and I never saw him again.

On August 8, 1960, I boarded the USS Lincoln County (LST-898), a landing ship tank built for the amphibious navy during World War II. She had just finished a tour in WestPac (West Pacific-Japan) and was running on a skeleton crew.

The messenger of the watch turned me over to the on-duty boatswain mate who took me below decks and assigned me a bunk with the "deck force." I was assigned the top bunk in the far corner of the compartment, next to a loud speaker. At first, I thought this would be a good location, out of the way. I unloaded my sea bag in my locker, took a tour of the ship, and was then dropped off at the mess hall for dinner. I didn't sleep well that first night, worrying about whether I would be accepted or not. Hell, they had to read that damn exam to me. Why was I here?

At 6:00 a.m., the loud speaker over my head sounded. "Now reveille, reveille, all hands heave out and trice-up (pull up the bottom-most bunk in the compartment so sweepers could sweep under them). Smoking lamp is lit in all berthing areas."

The words blasted in my ears. *Wow, what was that? What does that mean?* I put my head down on my pillow, listening to the sailors move about or go to the head (the bathroom). As I swung my legs over my bunk, the speaker sounded again. "Now, sweepers, man your brooms. Give a clean sweep down forward and aft. Empty all trash on the fantail."

The next thing I knew, I was swabbing the deck. Roll call was followed by a day of chipping paint, applying red lead primer, and covering the deck with haze-gray paint. The duty watch consisted of being messenger of the quarterdeck, a lookout, manning the helm, and boatswain locker duty, which consisted of line splicing and making knots like "fenders" and "monkey fists". I had no problems adapting to the duties of a deck hand or seaman apprentice (SA).

At the end of the day, or when pressure was more than I could endure, I escaped to either the boatswain or chain locker, where I practiced splicing line and other seaman-related hands-on work. This all paid off when the First Class Boatswain Mate had his deck force participate in a hands-on competition in line splicing and knot-tying. It wasn't long before I was winning all the competitions. I could tie a bowline in less than a second and make an eye splice within a minute, so I became the one to beat. I could throw a monkey fist farther and more accurately than any other seaman on the ship. I was shining, and I liked it. I felt respected.

One day while on liberty, a time when enlisted men could leave the ship, some of the older seamen got me "three sheets to the wind" drunk. I was seventeen and ended up in a tattoo parlor looking at tattoos. My shipmates thought that I should get a rabbit tattooed around my belly button with a grinning rabbit looking back over his shoulder, saying, "Kiss my ass."

Fortunately, I maintained enough sense to settle for a tattoo of a lone wolf on my upper left arm.

Though I was accepted and proving myself a hard worker, I preferred to be alone. With my new tattoo, I became known as Lone Wolf, and the nickname stuck with me until I left the ship.

My ship was to be decommissioned on March 24, 1961. They told all the SAs in deck force to study our seaman's manual, because we would be taking an advancement exam for seaman before receiving orders to a new duty station. I tried to make sense out of that manual. I knew some of the words, but most made no sense. Four and twenty black birds baked in the king's pie weren't enough to save me. I was the black sheep, and I had no wool to give. I was doomed, and I knew it.

I showed up in the mess hall along with four or five other SAs and sat down to take the exam. I stared at that exam, and again it was all multiple-choice questions. You would think that by now some combination of luck and odds would come my way, but not so. When the boatswain mate called for the test, I was less than halfway through it.

After he graded the exams, the boatswain was mad as hell. He accused me of getting drunk the night before or being downright derelict. He said that there was no excuse for failing that exam, that I knew that manual inside out, and my performance on deck was proof of that! He walked away, obviously disgusted.

Along with the other new seamen, I received orders for the USS Vernon County, ported out of Yokosuka,

Japan. My shipmates looked at me differently now; I was the only seaman apprentice on the ship, but I knew as much, if not more, than any of them. It was an awkward situation to be in, but a burden I knew well.

We were given leave before being shipped out to WestPac, and while I was home, my world came tumbling down around me.

My grandpa died of a heart attack. He was the only real father figure I ever had. My hero of heroes was gone.

He was born on April 14, 1886, in Newport Beach, Oregon. He was the child of a stump farmer and grew up using a chain, axe, and a stubborn mule to clear a forty-acre homestead of first-growth timber stumps (thus the term *stump farmer*). He served his country during World War I and did a little, or a lot, of bootlegging across the Canadian border during Prohibition (the little or a lot depended on his mood when spinning the yarn).

He gave me unconditional love. He believed in me and had complete confidence in my ability to overcome handicaps and succeed in life, and that was never so clear as when I attended his burial service. As I placed a red rose on his coffin, I realized the profound influence that he had had on my life. As I looked over his coffin and up to the sky, I knew that I was his signature on earth and heaven. *The die is cast,* I thought, *I am what I am. I am my grandpa's signature to mankind. I will succeed.* I knew that I had to jump back into "the box" and conquer my demons for him.

It was a good funeral. The pastor stumbled in pushing him on to heaven, but I'm certain that was because of

Grandpa's foul "mule-skinner" language, which he didn't hesitate to use when describing organized religion and its pastors.

Image 7 My Grandpa

11

Back in the Box

I caught a Greyhound to San Francisco where I met with several of my old shipmates. I noticed straight up that they were supporting seaman stripes on their shoulders. I still had my duce stripes indicating I was still an apprentice sailor, but also a newfound sense of courage from Grandpa's funeral.

We caught a Military Air Transport Service (MATS) flight to Yokosuka, Japan, and from there an Attack Transport to the Philippines, where we caught up with my new ship in Subic Bay, Olongapo, Philippines.

Olongapo was the most exciting port in the Orient but a questionable place for a new, eighteen-year-old sailor. I came off my ship and followed the smell of raw sewage to "shit river" and the base's main gate into town. Once across the bridge, I was greeted by the smell of street-side barbecues offering monkey meat on a stick. It was a good idea to decline all offers unless retuning to the ship with a dozen or so bottles of San Miguel beer or some Tanduay Rum in your gut. The aroma of "shit river" sewage, barbecued monkey, green San Miguel, cheap rum, the exhaust of jeepnies (the most popular means of transportation, made from U.S. surplus Jeeps left over from World War II), cheap perfume mixed, a never-ending array of Filipinas wearing thin cotton dresses—all that mixed, dashed, and blended with a salt breeze from Subic Bay, and you have Olongapo in May 1961.

We were in Subic Bay for about a week when we shipped out for our home port of Yokosuka, with an en route liberty stop at Okinawa that was spent avoiding fights with the Marines.

I liked Japan and spent my liberties mostly by myself walking the streets and riding the train to neighboring rural areas. I had adjusted well and was respected although I was still the lowest ranked sailor aboard ship. One day in June, I was approached by the ship's education officer and asked if I wanted to take a series of exams for a GED diploma. I agreed and went on base to take the tests, along with several other shipmates from the deck force. The tests were not supervised. The petty officer left the room, leaving us alone with the series of exams, which lasted for several days. I couldn't make heads or tails of the exam, so I copied my shipmate's answers and hoped for the best.

When we were later called on deck for a ceremony with the captain, he gave a speech, and we were issued our GEDs. I felt guilty for cheating. I remember looking at the piece of paper and noticing that the S for "Satisfactory Completion" was circled. I had cheated! It had no value. How was I worthy to be on life's path with stolen credentials?

I thought, The Little Red Hen's labor brought a loaf of bread from scattered grains of wheat. "Who will eat the bread?" asked The Little Red Hen. "We will," stated the three lazy bystanders. "Oh, no you won't," said the Little Red Hen, "I will." She did, sharing it with her own little family of chicks. Who am I to reap the reward of another's labor if I choose not to work?

Two or three months later, our second class boatswain mate told me that he was going to administer the seaman's exam to me. He said that I was "the best damn seaman on the ship" and deserved my stripes. He took me to the corner of the mess hall to give me the exam and said that he would return when the time was up, grade it, and issue my stripes. When he returned, he took one look at the exam and was mad as hell. I had failed.

He got right in my face with his anger, and for the second time in my life, I confessed that I couldn't read or write other than signing my name using my middle initial. I even confessed to cheating on the GED exam.

The boatswain called me back in December and told me that he had worked through a lot of red tape and received permission to readminister the exam. This time, he would read questions, give me multiple choices, and I could verbally choose an answer, just as I had done in boot camp.

I aced that exam! For two weeks, I strutted around the ship like a proud peacock.

A short time later, I was assigned to the captain's gig (private water taxi). I was a boatswain plus the coxswain (man in charge) of the captain's gig—damn, I was smoking hot and proud! It was interesting that nothing was ever said about cheating on the GED test.

All was going well until my sailor's cap showed up on my bunk, sliced by a knife and unwearable.

Without a cap, I would be out of uniform, which was a serious infraction. I wanted to find out who had done this and handle it personally. About a week after mail call, I returned to my bunk and saw one of my bunkmates reading a letter aloud to several other bunkmates. I thought nothing of it, but as I listened, I realized to my great surprise that he was reading one of *my* letters, a letter from my sister asking if I had any good-looking friends who would like to exchange letters with her. This was a letter that I had not been able to understand, and I had spent the last several days trying to figure out what my sister was talking about. I had left it on my bunk.

I demanded that the guy return my letter, but he laughed and continued reading, saying how stupid I was and that he was doing me a favor by reading it out loud so that I could understand it. We agreed that we would meet on the tank deck after taps (lights out) and fight it out.

Shortly after 10:00 p.m., we squared off with a good audience of onlookers. The fight lasted only a few seconds. The cap-slicing stopped, and no one ever teased me about my illiteracy again.

In February 1962, we were deployed to the island of Mindoro to participate in Operation Tulungan. En route we stopped in Okinawa, where we were to pick up a detachment of U.S. Marines. We deployed to an isolated village that technological advances had passed by. Other than duties related to the operation, we were restricted to the ship. I spent much of my off time on the fo'c'sle (foremost part of ship) to watch the village inhabitants go about their activities. I was drawn to the simplicity of their life in both dress and work. They did not challenge their environment but molded to it, allowing all creatures and plants to coexist. I longed to walk among them and learn more. My opportunity came when the captain requested his gig to go ashore. I was told to remain in sight of the gig while the captain conducted his business.

The jungle came up close to the village, and I could hear its life and smell its fragrances. I could not overcome its drawing power and silently stepped into its misty wonder where I could watch and not be seen. A sense of feral freedom overcame me. I was again "out of the box," looking in, in control. It was a wonderful state of power, and I wanted to stay with these people to live as they did, to dissolve into the village's nature. I saw my captain approaching the rustic pier where the gig was moored among the village dugouts and reluctantly stepped out of the green and back "into the box."

Operation Tulungan lasted about two months. We returned to Okinawa to drop off our detachment of Marines and receive some well-deserved liberty, but more Marines were waiting to board, this time an elite detachment of Marine RECON (reconnaissance). No reasons were given, nor were we given a destination. Like with my shipmates, I assumed that we were on an extended leg of the operation and headed back to

Mindoro. We were outside the harbor a few hours when I took over the helm and immediately knew that something was up. We were sailing solo, not on course toward Mindoro. I had the midnight-to-four watch that night, and when rotating up to the bridge at about 2:00 a.m., I saw the captain, the executive officer, the chief quartermaster, our chief boatswain mate, and our first-class radar man on the deck. A Russian destroyer was shadowing us.

Here we were, one lone 340-foot LST transport, loaded to the gills with elite Marine RECON, at the height of the Cold War, looking down the cannons of a Russian destroyer. We were in deep shit, and we knew it! We were like a mouse squeaking at a bear. During the day, the Russian destroyer cruised at variable distances off our starboard or port fantail. The Russian ship sped in close enough that we could make out the bridge, then would back off.

Unknown to our captain, his deck force, along with a few gunners mates, gathered at the fantail (back end of ship) to provide some balance to this standoff. We flipped off their bridge when we saw through our binoculars that they were looking at us, and we pulled down our pants and mooned that Russian Bear with the most beautiful array of white and black asses their Communist eyes had ever be held. (I doubt that in 1962 any of the Russian sailors had ever seen a black ass.)

Working closely with Marine RECON, we learned that we were running hot (live munitions on board). We stopped flipping off and mooning the Russians. I imagined my white ass filling up the crosshairs of a Russian cannon.

The mouse-and-bear game went on for several days until we set a northern course and started picking up traffic, which consisted mostly of fishing boats. We were in the Gulf of Thailand when the captain called us to the main deck and announced that we would be heading up the Bangkok River and docking in Bangkok. It was made clear that this was a goodwill visit and we were the first U.S. military ship to visit the Port of Bangkok since World War II. We would be in port for only one week and were restricted to "Cinderella liberty" (liberty that ends at midnight). This announcement caused a stir among the crew. If it was truly a goodwill tour, why the presence of Marines running hot munitions, and why were we being shadowed by the Russian Navy? Years later, I learned that President Kennedy was sending our first troops into Vietnam and using Thailand as a back door.

This is a report of the examinee's achievement in a recently completed USAFI test. It is accompanied by a Certificate of Completion when the examinee has satisfactorily completed a USAFI course in which he enrolled or has satisfactorily completed all parts of the high school level General Educational Development test battery. The examinee's copy of this report and the certificate, if included, should be presented to the examinee. The report is forwarded for entry in the examinee's official military record.

CO (I&E Off.)
Test Sec 10
US Nav El, Spt Act Box 31 Navy 3923   USS Vernon County (LST-1161)
FPO San Francisco, Calif.   FPO San Francisco, Calif.

EXAMINEE'S NAME   Rodney F. Williams, SN   SERVICE NO.   USN 5450467   GR. OF SERVICE   N

DATE COMPLETED		TEST FORM	HIGH SCHOOL LEVEL GENERAL EDUCATIONAL DEVELOPMENT TESTS														RATING CODE
NO.	YR.		TEST 1 STD SCORE	U.S. PCT.	TEST 2 STD SCORE	U.S. PCT.	TEST 3 STD SCORE	U.S. PCT.	TEST 4 STD SCORE	U.S. PCT.	TEST 5 STD SCORE	U.S. PCT.				
6	61	M	37	10	37	10	40	16	42	21	50	50			S	S—SATISFACTORY
																U—UNSATISFACTORY
																I—INCOMPLETE

DATE COMPLETED		TEST FORM	COLLEGE LEVEL GENERAL EDUCATIONAL DEVELOPMENT TESTS											RATING CODE
NO.	YR.		TEST 1 STD SCORE	U.S. PCT.	TEST 2 STD SCORE	U.S. PCT.	TEST 3 STD SCORE	U.S. PCT.	TEST 4 STD SCORE	U.S. PCT.			
NO ENTRY														S—SATISFACTORY
														U—UNSATISFACTORY

DATE COMPLETED		NUMBER AND TITLE OF COURSE OR TEST		RATING CODE
NO.	YR.			
NO ENTRY				H—WITH DISTINCTION
				S—SATISFACTORY
				U—UNSATISFACTORY

* THIS BLOCK IDENTIFIED A RETEST. 1—1ST RETEST, 2 2ND RETEST.

James A. Larkin
JAMES A. LARKIN
DIRECTOR

USAFI FORM T-48 (REV) MAY 61   EXAMINEE'S COPY
(SEE REVERSE SIDE)

United States Armed Forces Institute
JAPAN

This is to certify that

Rodney F. Williams, SN

has successfully completed the USAFI

TESTS OF GENERAL EDUCATIONAL DEVELOPMENT
HIGH SCHOOL LEVEL

this date   22 June 1961   service no.   USN 5450467

Image 8 My first GED that I cheated on, still got terrible scores, yet was given a "Satisfactory" passing mark. Karma had it that this certificate could not be found in 1971 when I was required to obtain a new one, honestly.

12
Rub-A-Dub-Dub

I was fascinated with Bangkok. Its people and scenery were beautiful.

We hit the port of entry running. Our Marines were unloaded under tight security and rushed off, not to be seen again. A "scuttlebutt" or cold-water fountain was located on the ship's fantail, and within hours of docking, children and young adults found out about the liberal source of cold water. They tied their dinghies to our stern anchor and used the anchor as a ladder to climb aboard and get a drink of water. That was the sum of the goodwill portion of our tour that I observed.

One of the big perks about being assigned to the captain's gig was that you got to knock off work at noon. There I was, nineteen years old and coming off the ship at noon in full uniform in a port that had not seen uniformed American sailors since World War II.

I hit the beach with $4.50 in my pocket and started walking and watching the people with fascination. The side streets were filled with naked children, as innocent and free as nature itself, and orange-clad Buddhist monks, holding bowls and talking to people. Everyone stared at me and acted like they would like to talk to me but didn't know how to go about it. I felt like a creature in a zoo that others were entertained by.

When waiting to cross the street, a young man approached me, and in broken English, asked if I needed help. He then led me to what he swore to be the best restaurant in Bangkok, and I learned that it belonged to his family. His sister, an English student at a nearby school, was the most beautiful young lady that anyone could behold. She stood behind the counter and introduced herself with a name that was so long you could put the alphabet into it twice and still have room left. Seeing how confused I was and how I struggled to get my tongue around her name, she shortened it to Dawg. The most beautiful young lady in the world had a first name pronounced as *dog*. I was fed a delicious dinner, served the best beer in the house, and flooded with instant friends and questions.

"Have you met President Kennedy?"

"No," I said, confused.

"USA good, President Kennedy good man, he save Southeast Asia. He sends in the Marines just like John Wayne."

I thought, So much for our visit to promote peace and goodwill. These people know more about what is going on than I do.

There were several European customers in the restaurant, and their comments went something like this: "Damn you Americans and your #%@$ President Kennedy. He sacrificed all those young fighting men in Cuba at the Bay of Pigs, and now he's going to do the same with Vietnam. Take your Marines and go home!" It felt like I was set on a pedestal as the spokesman for a master race.

At that time, my life consisted of getting my monthly paycheck, surviving a few poker games, buying some beer, and hoping to have enough money left over to spend on pretty girls. I had in my sights the most beautiful of them all.

I spent the rest of the week with Dawg, her brother, and parents. I got to know the whole family, as they took me in like a long-lost son. I went on two dates with Dawg, always accompanied by her brother, which was the custom, and just before shipping out, I proposed to her in front of the whole family. She accepted, along with the rest of the family and witnessed by the lizards that climbed up and down the walls.

My ship left Bangkok at the end of the week. Dawg and I agreed to wait until I returned to the States before starting the paperwork for the marriage and her immigration to the United States.

While en route to our home port of Yokosuka, we were hit by a horrendous storm with high winds and a raging sea that sounded like a freight train roaring down a track. It was so violent that we had to strap ourselves into our bunks. The ship crashed on the sea with such force that it caused the ship to shudder as if it would break apart.

I was called to the bridge to man the helm in the wheelhouse, with the captain and chief quartermaster present. The captain ordered me to the helm and gave me a course that would put our bow directly into the storm and oncoming waves. I relieved the helmsman and strapped myself to the helm. I looked down and saw that I was standing in the sloshing vomit of the helmsman that I had just relieved. I set my helm to the course that the captain had ordered. Because it was a flat-bottomed ship, and even though the ballast tanks were full to allow us to ride the sea better, it was difficult to keep the bow securely directed into the storm. The ship surged with the storm; its stern lifted as the bow dipped. The ship floundered from port to starboard and back again.

The captain yelled above the storm, "Make her answer her helm, seaman!"

As I swung the helm from port to starboard and back, I found myself talking to my ship as if it were alive: "Come on, Lady, we can do this, answer your helm." I spotted a monster rogue wave. We rode up the wall of the nearly vertical wave, and I heard the captain shout, "The ship is yours—don't broach her!"

We were engulfed by the rogue wave as it crashed down on us. The wheelhouse was flooded, and the ship yawed violently to starboard and into the crouch of the tempest. I was running on pure adrenaline as I brought the helm to hard port and heard myself yell, "Answer your helm, Lady, and come to port!" I knew that every person aboard depended on me to not broach our ship.

The rogue wave passed over us, and we surfaced like a submarine. The captain and I looked at each other with fear on our faces. We fought the storm through the night until the morning hours when the storm finally let up. I bonded with my captain that night, which would benefit me in the near future. From that day on, I saw the ship as much more than steel and paint and took pride in caring for her.

Stopping at the commercial seaport of Shimizu, Japan, we dropped anchor about a hundred yards off the stern of a Russian merchant ship, also anchored waiting for pier space, at about 10:00 a.m. Other merchant ships from Germany, Greece, and Sweden were in the harbor, tied to the pier. This was the perfect storm for a cocky, arrogant sailor who was about to be humbled.

I caught the first liberty boat at noon and was the only enlisted man to hit the beach at that hour—the first of several mistakes. This was a merchant seaman's port, not a U.S. Navy port. There was no Shore Patrol (SP) to keep young, arrogant sailors in line. We had just been paid, so I had what I felt was enough money in my pocket to have a few drinks, get something to eat, and head back to the ship. I walked toward the waterfront bars, not realizing that a liberty port that hadn't seen U.S. military since World War II and a bar full of merchant sailors was not a good mix.

By 12:30, I found myself in a bar full of German Merchant Marines. I was in full summer uniform and was welcomed to their table. They were drinking Vodka Screwdrivers, a mixture of orange juice and vodka, so I ordered the same. This was my second mistake.

It soon became clear that "the mess cook had fed me a double portion of dumb for breakfast that morning." The Screwdrivers took hold of me quickly. Before I knew it, I was out of money, so I traded my sailor's cap for another Screwdriver—then my neckerchief—then my jumper. I swapped half my uniform for drinks and suddenly realized that I was sitting at a table of drunken Germans, trying to understand what limited English was being said.

I found myself walking up the gangplank to board the German merchant ship with my new friends. When we went below deck, an officer informed me that they were preparing to get under way and if I didn't want to go to Hamburg, I had to disembark immediately. I was able to retrieve my uniform and was soon back on the waterfront.

The next bar that I went to was full of Swedes; a neighboring bar was full of Greeks. I again traded pieces of my uniform for drinks, even though I knew that being out of uniform was a serious offense.

The sun had gone down. The bars would be closing, and I would have to catch the liberty boat back to my ship. A racket erupted in the street, and the bar patrons dashed out to the waterfront to watch a big fight between some Greek and Swedish sailors. I joined in and, to the best of my memory and what my shipmates told me, gave a pretty good accounting of myself. The police broke up the fight, and we all returned to our respective bars. Impressed that I had fought for them, my Swedish friends toasted me. My uniform was returned in full, and it was a good thing that I hadn't worn it during the fight. I had a fat lip, a cut underneath my left eye, and blood all over my t-shirt. We all went on drinking, singing, and arm wrestling for drinks.

There I was representing the U.S. Navy in a disoriented uniform with three Swedes, all four of us stumbling around the waterfront. I had an hour before the last liberty launch was to arrive, so what could four drunken sailors do for an hour? We happened upon a pier and found an unmanned row boat with oars and several grappling hooks (an anchor with several claws attached to a line).

The four of us boarded the boat and rowed out into a moonlit bay where we noticed that the Russian merchant ship was still flying its colors (its country flag) on the fantail. It was not uncommon for a smaller merchant ship to fly its colors on the fantail rather than from the bridge.

I decided that I wanted the flag for a souvenir and convinced my new Swedish friends to assist me. We rowed, as silently as drunken sailors could, to the stern of the ship. Having not yet unloaded its cargo, it was riding low in the water, allowing a sober sailor an excellent opportunity to board it. I was not sober.

I looked at the five-pointed star sitting on top of the hammer and sickle with its red background, waving in the moonlit breeze. I knew I had to have it.

We decided that the best way to board would be to secure one of the grappling hooks to the fantail. I would climb aboard, retrieve the Russian flag, climb back down, and we would row away.

I stood on the bow of the row boat like a whaler about to harpoon a whale, only I had a grappling hook, and my whale was a Russian merchant ship. It took me three throws and a lot of clanging before I secured the grappling hook. With the hook secure, I began to climb up the line. I heard loud voices above me and looked up to see several Russian sailors yelling at me and motioning for me to board while one pointed a revolver at my head. I looked down expecting to see my Swedish friends and the row boat to rescue me. Not so. The three of them were rowing as fast as they could in full retreat to the safety of the pier. I heard my captain over the loud speaker: "Stand to, sailor, and await to be picked up!"

The sound of my captain's voice sobered me up quickly. I looked up to see the revolver still pointed at my head and the Russian sailors still yelling and, I assumed by their hand motions, ordering me to board. I looked back down and knew what I had to do. SPLASH!

I came to the surface to hear the davits on my ship - a device used to lower a small boat from the ship - it was lowering an amphibious landing craft to rescue me. I kicked off my shoes and swam as fast as I could toward my ship and the brig that was awaiting me, praying that I wouldn't be shot first. Better a Navy brig than a Russian brig.

Image 9 On leave from boot camp.

13
Old King Cole

My actions of that night were to be kept out of sight and out of mind for political reasons, so it did not go on my record. I did get the biggest "ass-chewing lecture" a hung-over sailor ever received. The captain assigned me ninety days' restriction to the ship with hard labor, which equated to twelve to sixteen hours hard labor per day, seven days a week, for ninety days. I was fired from the captain's gig and assigned to the paint locker.

When we arrived back in Yokosuka, a letter from Dawg was waiting for me. Between my inability to read and her limited English, I was not able to make much from her letter except that she was anxious to get married and get the immigration papers filed. I slept with her letter under my pillow for weeks, trying to figure out how to answer it. With the help of a trusted friend, I finally got a letter off to her, and it was decided in a roundabout way that we would wait until I was about to leave the Navy before starting the paperwork.

The hard labor did its job. I was humbled, pliable as soft clay and ready to be molded into something better than what I had been. My liberty was renewed but restricted to the weekends and on base for two months, a kind of captain's probation. With no off-base liberty to distract me and released from hard labor, I was left with a lot of free time.

I missed my nursery rhymes and comic books, but even if I had access to them, it would not have been enough. I needed more. That spark deep within my soul was glowing. I needed to be challenged, like a fisherman wanting to catch an even bigger fish. I was Simple Simon, wanting to catch a whale yet still restricted to no more than his mother's pail. I yearned to read.

I found myself walking past the base library as I had many times before, but now a force pulled me to the stairs toward the formidable double doors. Would they intimidate me, stop me before I could enter? Not this time!

Years later, I wrote the following in my journal:

My destiny that day no power could stop
My soul was afire from a spark so faint

I said to myself with determined strength
I CAN!

At that very moment my third eye did see
The arm of one long past and dead poet (Walter Malone)

He did grasp me to hold me firm
His voice did whisper great words to me

"Though deep in mire, wring not your hands
and weep;
I lend my arm to all who say I CAN!
No shame-faced outcast ever sank so deep
But yet might rise and be again a man!

For behold through those doors is your ocean
An ocean full of whales
Simple Simon you shall be no more
Now go catch your whale!"

I ascended the stairs and entered the library to behold my ocean full of whales.

I stood before the librarian and asked her if there was a book there that would teach me how to read. She looked at me oddly, as if wondering how I could read a book to teach me to read! Perception, patience, and wisdom blessed this librarian. Before I knew it, we sat at one of the tables, and she began teaching me how to read.

Even after coming off base restriction, I continued to spend my free time at the library. I learned to identify a vowel from a consonant and how to break a word into syllables, much like the way my little sister had taught me in eighth grade. This helped me tremendously, but what I needed was a speech therapist. My pronunciation was horrible. Try as I may, I was not able to correctly pronounce letters, or groups of letters, or blend sounds to properly pronounce the unidentified words that I saw in books. I felt like the boy on page 25 of *The Child's World*, walking up that lonely path to a red schoolhouse with a bag full of books, stuck between ten o'clock and noon.

I created a phonics pattern that tapped into my ability to pronounce words. If I didn't know the correct pronunciation of a word, I slurred the sounds together, and it worked; I had my own language to work from. I started with comic books like Mickey Mouse, Donald Duck, Goofy, my favorite Li'l Abner, and my friend Joe Btfsplk. I depended mostly on the pictures, but slowly the words began to come to me, enough so that I could somewhat put the words to what was displayed by the cartoonist.

I thanked the librarian for her help. Spreading my arms and looking about, I asked, "Are there any books here that talk about slugs eating dead mice?" Again, she looked at me with her head slightly cocked.

"I don't think so. Why would slugs eat dead mice? They're vegetarians."

"I was just wondering if there was such a book on that subject."

She smiled. "No, I'm sorry, I don't believe there is."

I walked out of the library with a smile. Wow, I believe I am the only one in the whole world that knows that slugs eat dead mice!

While we were in Okinawa, I got a telegram from Mom stating that Jack Brosig had died of a massive heart attack. I didn't feel any remorse for his passing; in fact, I felt relief, knowing that my siblings and mom were no longer subject to his abuse.

When I was offered a transfer to the Naval Amphibious Base in Coronado, California, I was torn as to what to do. I was comfortable with my environment, I liked my ship and shipmates, I liked Japan, and I was in love. I was spending my free time learning, with my ocean full of whales. Why go back to the States and people who saw me as retarded?

I decided to accept the transfer and caught a MATS flight to Tokyo, then a commercial civilian flight to San Francisco. Upon landing, I felt the same desperate feeling that I'd had before shipping out to Japan. I felt out of my element. In Japan and aboard my ship, I had a structure to follow; I was a hands-on seaman and accepted well enough by my peers. Now that I was home, I wanted to break free. It was tempting to just up and disappear.

At a new duty station, I would have to adjust all over again. I was tempted to visit the "jungle" and see who might be hanging out but instead went to Hogback Mountain to spend a couple of solitary days, thinking. I was glad to see that my cache was still intact. It lifted my spirits to know that if all failed, I had what I really wanted in life, waiting for me. The essentials in my cache—a portable shelter, food, warm clothing, fire, hemp line, fishing gear, a good knife, and a few other odd and ends—would allow me to survive.

At Mom's house, I spotted something on the bottom shelf of a bookcase: *The Wahoo Bobcat*. Just seeing the cover excited me, and I was off to a quiet place to hold the book in my hand. It felt alive with energy. It's spirit was calling me. I felt excited and scared at the same time:

scared because at twenty years old, I feared that I would not understand what was there. As I slowly opened the book, I turned past the table of contents and illustrations to the preface. Tears welled in my eyes, and a great joy swelled up inside me. It was no longer foreign. It was alive. It spoke to me in big letters, "Pre-face." It spoke again, "For years I fol-lowed the tra-cks, the Wa-hoo Ti-ger's."

I had a key, a living key that opened knowledge and allowed me to see the light of the world. These keys consisted of three building blocks: vowels, consonants, and syllables. With these new friends, I began a process that would eventually lead me to what I am today. Simple Simon had hooked his whale, and now he just had to reel him in.

I moved on to understand what this wonderful book wanted to tell me. "And once (which I pronounced *wons*) I—" My heart dropped. I couldn't make any sense of the word *caught*.

I went looking for my sister, and she said, "It's *caught*, like in 'you caught a ball,'" she pointed to the word, "or caught a glimpse."

"How do you pronounce the *gh*?" I asked.

"You don't. It's silent."

"Silent? Why would anyone want to put letters in a word and not use them? That's stupid. Just spell it *caut*!"

She shrugged her shoulders as she walked away. "I don't know. My teacher says it's the king's language, so go ask the king."

"The king of what?"

"The King of England, who else?" She hollered from her bedroom.

"What a dumb king," I mumbled as I retreated to my room.

This king didn't know what he was doing, and his obedient serfs didn't have the guts to set him straight. I thought, *Maybe it was Old King Cole and his fiddlers three. Yeah, that's it!* The poem I had learned at my mother's side came easily.

I reimagined this problem into something that I could get my head around and imagined the full story.

Old King Cole was truly a merry old soul, and he told his fiddlers three that "g" and "h" were two tired, old consonants that needed a place to sleep. *Go forth, my fiddlers three, and catch "g" and "h" and bring them to me.*

The obedient fiddlers went forth to find "g" and "h" and found them. On their way home, the fiddlers came across Little Boy Blue, fast asleep under the haycock. "Little Boy Blue," they hollered, "come blow your horn! The King's sheep are in the meadow, his cows are in the corn."

Still Little Boy Blue slept on.

"Shall we go over and wake him?" asked one of the fiddlers.

"No," said another, "for he be sure to cry."

The fiddlers came to the king and presented "g" and "h." They also explained that his sheep were in the meadow, his cows were in the corn, and Little Boy Blue was under the haycock fast asleep.

Old King Cole pondered this news with great concern. "If Little Boy Blue had been awake, he would have *caut* the sheep before they got into my meadow, and he would have *caut* the cows before they got into my corn. I see that "g" and "h" need a place where they can sleep well, so fiddlers, put them in *caut*."

The fiddlers placed "g" and "h" in *caut* so that they could sleep well and not worry about being caught ever again.

Old King Cole sat back in his chair and thout, What a dastardly deed I did give the world this day. Where else can I put "g" and "h" to make them as quiet and lazy as can be?

The king *thout* of another place to put "g" and "h" to further confuse the King's Language. To this day, to be *caught* up with the very *thought* of "g" and "h" reminds me of Old King Cole and his fiddlers three.

I was proud of myself when I turned out the lights that night. I had managed to get through the preface and first chapter. The last time I held the book, in eighth grade, I had not been able to get past the first sentence and needed my mom or sister to read it to me.

I met my sister's best friend, Dolly, and realized that I wasn't ready for Dawg. It was not a difficult decision, and I took the coward's way out: I used my weakness in writing as my excuse for not answering her letters.

The remainder of my leave was spent getting to know Dolly. I did my best to portray myself as confident, mature, and as she told me many years later, "a bit sophisticated." No matter how I appeared on the surface,

I felt unworthy of her. I could barely read or able to write—how was I going to get a job that enabled me to support such a beautiful woman?

When it was time to report for duty, she met me at the bus depot to see me off and asked me to write to her. I agreed, knowing I could not accomplish such a task unless I had help. We waved at each other as the bus pulled out, and I wondered, as I sat back in my seat, if I would ever be worthy to fall in love with someone as precious as Dolly.

I reported for duty and was assigned to Assault Craft Unit One (ACU-1) with less than a year left to serve. During that time, I hitchhiked from San Diego to Klamath Falls and to Medford, Oregon. Both times, I met up with Dolly, but kept her at a distance. I never allowed her to know what was going on inside me.

On November 22, 1963, President Kennedy was assassinated, and on December 19, 1963, I received an honorable discharge from the Navy.

While sitting on a Greyhound bus, headed for home, I saw a freight train that appeared to be cannon-balling north, and I couldn't help but think of the advice I received from the hobo. Yes, it had been a good ride for four years.

Image 10   My imagination of Old King Cole

14
Ruse

Tom, Tom, the piper's son,
Stole a pig and away he run!
The pig was eat, and Tom was beat,
And Tom went roaring down the street.
(Bjoland, 35)

On December 20, 1963, I stood outside the bus depot in Medford, Oregon, breathing in the crisp morning air, waiting for my brother, Rick, to pick me up.

It was good that Mom had moved to Medford, because it separated me from two temptations that I didn't need: my hobo jungle and my cache on Hogback Mountain. I immediately applied for a driver's license. I passed the written portion after my third attempt and passed the driving portion without incident. I pulled money out of savings, caught a Greyhound to Portland, and went shopping for a used car with my dad. Dad really pulled through for me—I bought a 1956 Pontiac for $105. A week later, I drove back to Medford to start looking for a job.

Job hunting proved to be more difficult than I thought. I showed up in my white shirt, tie, and sport coat, looking sharp. When a potential employer handed me an application, I said that I had another appointment in the next few minutes and would bring it back the next day. I took it home and recruited my mom or sister to help me fill it out.

In most cases, I was called for an interview and given more paperwork to fill out on the spot. The problem was that I could not spell or write a comprehensive sentence. The employers were always nice when telling me that they would keep my application on file or call when or if needed.

No one would hire me. I handled the rejection by again entertaining my escape from society. The thought gave me a surge of energy that boosted my self-esteem. (Even now, when I'm in the wilderness in total solitude, I don't sell myself out. A feral environment provides me with the confidence I need and when I need it the most! I can always count on it being there.)

One night while out drinking, which was always by myself, I met an older man who worked for the Bureau of Land Management (BLM). The more we drank, the more we talked, and I took in everything he had to say. He was a close friend of the director of the BLM in Coos Bay, Oregon, who was a close friend of the district director of the BLM in Medford. By the time the evening was over, I knew the complete biography of the Coos Bay office director and his family.

The next morning, I showed up on the doorstep of the Medford branch of the BLM in my white shirt, tie, and Old Spice aftershave, ready to make an impression.

I walked in like I owned the place and asked for the district director by name. The secretary looked me over and asked my name, which I confidently gave, along with the name of the director at the home office in Coos Bay who had "invited me to drop by." I was asked to take a seat. Before I could pick up a magazine, the district director came out, shook my hand, slapped me on the shoulder, invited me into his office, sat me down at his desk, and told his secretary to bring me a cup of coffee.

I realized what I was stepping into: there was no way that I was going to get away with the ruse of being a friend of the director's colleague without getting my royal, Irish ass kicked. We made small talk about our supposedly mutual good friend and his family in Coos Bay, but when we ran out of small talk, the district director hinted that he needed to get back to work and asked if there was anything else. I took a deep breath.

"Well, sir, I'm looking for work."

He looked confused and then said with a shrug, "Okay, what kind of work are you looking for?"

"Anything ya got."

He leaned on his elbows. "Anything, huh? Let's see, there should be something out there. I'll have the secretary give you an application to fill out, and we'll see what we have."

He got up, picked up a six-page government employment application, sat me down at a table, and handed me the application. Looking at the application, I knew that I was caught. I said that I would take it home to fill it out because I had "stuff" at my house that I needed to reference. He insisted that I fill it out as best I could. He wanted to "get right on it."

Shit happens, and when it does, you usually bring it on yourself.

In less than fifteen minutes, the district director returned to inform me that his good friend in Coos Bay had never heard of me. He escorted me out the front door and closed it without a goodbye or good luck. If I had gone into the office and mentioned the name of the man who had recommended that I drop by, who knows what would have happened. At least I would not have been shown the door with my self-respect in the gutter.

Why didn't I tell the truth? I had many years of experience at finding ways to navigate in a literate society. I had made it a habit to improvise and portray myself as something that I wasn't.

I was angry that day when the BLM district director rightfully closed the door behind me. I was angry at everything inside "the box" that I wanted but couldn't get to. The truth was that I wasn't ready to work for the BLM, or any other company, as long as I felt that I had to fake my identity to achieve my goals.

My Uncle Walter, who was the assistant general manager for Bethlehem Steel in Seattle, came to my rescue. He offered me a job for $2.10 per hour, and I was off to Seattle.

15

The Nut House

In early 1964, I arrived in Seattle to work in Bethlehem Steel's Nut and Bolt factory, nicknamed the "Nut House." I rented a small flat overlooking the south end of California Avenue in West Seattle.

Bethlehem Steel was a good place for a young, broad-shouldered man to start out. The work was hard, and the pay was adequate. I was part of what Mr. Prazenski called his personal "labor pool" that he moved around where he thought best. After a couple of weeks, he asked me if I would like to work on the track spike machine, making railroad spikes. I would get one hour of overtime pay each day and additional piece work over my hourly pay.

I didn't hesitate for the chance to improve my pay status and wondered why I was being offered the position, having been employed for only a few weeks. I soon learned that this was the most dangerous job in the shop. I found out the hard way after literally burning my pants off my body one day.

The hard work was good for me. At the end of the day, our track spike team and the other steel workers met at the Red Feather Tavern to have a few cold beers and play twenty-five-cent pool. When I arrived at home, I showered, watched the news, fixed dinner, watched some television, and went to bed.

On payday, I went to the Double Eagle Tavern or the Red Feather Tavern to cash my paycheck, and I did everything in cash. Banks intimidated me.

With the success and esteem that employment was giving me, I decided it was time to find a wife. I was making good money, had my own place, and could support a family. The question was who, and the answer was simple. Dolly!

While my mates and I were watching a football game and wondering what we were going to do over the three-day weekend, I interrupted the game with an announcement. "I'm leaving in the next few minutes for Klamath Falls to marry Dolly." I explained who Dolly was and what she meant to me. My sister had informed me that she had a boyfriend named Gary who I would have to "whip" while I was there.

My friend, Don, said, "You're telling us that you're heading out for Klamath Falls to beat up this guy named Gary, bring *his* girlfriend back here to Seattle, and marry her, all in the next three days?"

"That's the plan."

"What if she has a different perspective on all this?"

"What do you mean by perspective?"

Don explained the meaning of *perspective*.

I addressed the attentive group. "You know that movie where the Arab on a white stallion comes galloping down the beach, with his cape flying in the

124

wind, and reaches down and swoops up his damsel in distress and flings her onto his steed, and the two go galloping off into the sunset?" Staring in wonderment, my friends nodded. "That's what I intend to do after I take care of business with this Gary. I had an opportunity to whip his ass a long time ago and should have done it then." I left with instructions to turn off the lights and lock up after they left.

I threw a change of clothes into the back seat of my newly purchased 1956 Oldsmobile and headed south for Klamath Falls. The drive gave me time to think things over. Would I offend Dolly if I flew into her life like this? What if she really did love this Gary? Was I entertaining thoughts of grandeur to believe that someone as beautiful as Dolly would want to marry a high-school dropout who could barely read and was unable to write?

I arrived at my sister's house in Klamath Falls, and Dolly was there, either by coincidence or my sister's manipulation. I melted like butter, and my stomach was dancing somewhere between my esophagus and huevos.

It was a friendly weekend that went nowhere. I found myself back on the interstate headed for Seattle, alone. It would be forty-five years before I spoke to Dolly again.

One day, I was invited to a party at a friend's home. Two pretty young women were there, one a friend of the host who invited me. When I asked the prettier of the two if she would like to dance, her eyes lit up, she said yes, and away we went.

Wow! She was educated, refined, and a college graduate. This lady could teach me to read better, write, and do arithmetic. I asked her out, and she accepted.

Before long, we were in front of the Justice of the Peace, getting married, and I had to tell her that I was in the early stages of overcoming illiteracy.

We had opened a checking account and got a Bon Marche credit card—I didn't even know what a credit card was. I turned over my paycheck to her along with all the financial decisions. When we found out that she was pregnant, she quit her job to be a stay-at-home mom.

One day, she put the checkbook in my shirt pocket and sent me to an auto service shop to pay for some tires. The service attendant handed me a bill for about $20. I didn't have $20 in my wallet, and I had a checkbook but absolutely no idea how to use it. I told the man that I was about $5 short and would leave my spare tire as collateral until I could go home and get more money. He said that my wife had called earlier and arranged for me to pay for the tires with a check, motioning to the checkbook in my shirt pocket. Eventually, he said that he would take the tires off the car and charge me extra to put them back on if I decided to leave without paying up front. I said okay, asked for a pen, and excused myself to the bathroom.

I sat in the bathroom, staring at that checkbook, scared to death.

I was able to figure out where the number amount went and where the written amount went. I managed the number amount but had no idea how to write the number 20, much less the name of the business. I guessed that I had the right location for my signature, which I could write as long as I didn't have to include my middle name.

When I finally came out of the restroom, I sheepishly handed the check to the attendant who looked at it, frowned, and said that he could not accept it. I shrugged, not knowing what else to do, but he asked if it would be okay if he wrote it out and I signed it. I agreed and handed him the checkbook. He looked at the balance page, tore out my miserable first attempt at writing the check, and said that I would need to void it (whatever that meant). He wrote the check, had me sign it, and handed the checkbook back to me, reminding me that I would have to subtract it from my balance sheet. I had no idea what he was talking about.

Once home, I handed my wife the checkbook and said nothing about what had happened.

On August 8, 1965, my wife gave birth to a healthy baby boy. We named him David Mark, and my life had new purpose. I liked family life, and I really wanted to make it, to be like everyone else.

I read the Sunday funnies and, on my breaks at work, read comic books and simple novels about nature. It was slow progress, but I was beginning to fear that the slow pace of my learning was going to outlive me. I needed to speed things up.

I contacted Seattle Central Community College, picked up an enrollment booklet, and when I thought I was signing up for a course in English grammar, I ended up in Algebra I. Wow, that was a shock on my first day of class. My biggest challenge was reading the questions well enough to understand.

I hadn't been in the class more than a few weeks when I got into an argument with my wife. I left the house to cool off and came back to find her parents moving her out.

Just like that, my wife was gone, along with my little boy. She filed for a divorce; I countered by requesting that the court mandate counseling. The court complied, and we received a court order that required us to attend marriage counseling. The day came, and there we sat in a meeting room. The counselor came in, handed us pencils and pads of paper and asked us to write our reasons for this separation. My wife began writing with a smile.

I stared at a blank pad of paper and knew what I wanted to write but didn't know how to do it.

Damn, damn, damn, my bad luck.

I wasn't going to hand in a blank sheet of paper, so I gave it my best effort. My statement went somewhat like this: "The rason im hear is bicaus I lov my wyfe and sun and wont to meak our marag work."

In the end, a Catholic judge denied the divorce. In retaliation, my wife maxed out the Bon Marche credit card. When the judge said that I couldn't make her live with me and that I was responsible for her debt, I told the judge to grant her the divorce.

I had lost my family, my reason to succeed. You would have thought that I would have run off hoboin', "gone feral," or something of that sort, but I liked my job, and I was in a good working environment. I had tasted the fruits of literacy enough to want more.

I didn't sacrifice night school, but on weekends I went to the waterfront, walked into a tavern, hunting for bullies, and when I found one, sat back and watched him. When he got too arrogant and picked on or belittled someone smaller than himself, I walked up to him, gave him a shove, and challenged him to pick on someone his own size.

It worked like a straight flush in five-card stud. We were at it, over the tables on the floor rolling in the beer and dirt. The fight was generally broken up before anyone was seriously hurt, but if it went out to the parking lot, a circle of onlookers accompanied us, and my boxing and wrestling skills kicked in. With at least a six-pack of beer in us, we were unable to do much damage other than a split lip, black eye, or bloody nose. The bottom line was this: who is the better person, the bully or the bully of the bully?

With this going on, I managed to keep attending my algebra class. Even though the instructor wrote formulas on the board that I couldn't understand, and with no one outside the classroom to help me, I was lost but was determined to succeed. If I was going down in this class, I was going down with the gloves off, fighting!

When the course was complete, the instructor called me into his office to get my grade. I arrived with butterflies whirling in my stomach. To my great surprise and inexpressible joy, I passed the class with a C-. Wow! I passed! The instructor explained that he would have given me a C or B- if I had used the algebra formulas to figure my answers. I admitted that I was not able to understand the formulas that he put on the blackboard and so made up my own; I got more than 75 percent of the problems correct by "coming through the back door." My instructor complimented me on a job well done but stood by his word that algebra was all about the formula to figure the problem.

So be it. I, Rodney Frank Williams, had passed an algebra course, and I did it without cheating—I didn't even glance at another student's test or worksheet! It was my grade, and I had earned it.

16
Light!

Art thou a mourner? Rouse thee from thy spell;
Art thou a sinner? Sins may be forgiven;
Each morning gives thee wings to flee from hell,
Each night a star to guide thy feet to heaven.
(Rittenhouse)

I was twenty-three during the summer of 1966 and living a hard, fast life of drinking and fighting with bullies, but I also picked up a hobby of scuba diving on my days off.

One Sunday afternoon, I was scuba diving with a companion in the Hood Canal, looking for octopus. We were diving deeper than I had ever been. We had been down for some time, not having any luck, and were due to surface. I didn't realize that the J-valve on my tank had gotten caught in my weight belt and was in an open position. (The J-valve maintained a reserve of air needed for a normal ascent.)

When I realized my predicament, it was too late. All my air had been used up.

Every fiber of my being was screaming to jolt to the surface. My partner was ten to fifteen feet below me, and I knew that I was at seventy-five to one hundred feet deep. To jolt to the surface would cause "the bends," which would cripple me for life or kill me.

I called upon my God as best I knew. With all the faith and limited knowledge of what Mrs. Peach had taught me, I dove even deeper to catch up with my diving partner. He was cruising through the bottom rocks looking for places where an octopus might be hiding. My lungs were screaming; I was quickly using up the reserves in my lungs and blood with the additional effort. As I started to grab his fin, my mask filled with blood and saltwater, impairing my vision. In my panic, I had neglected to equalize the pressure in my sinus cavities, causing them to rupture.

Blindly, I kicked forward, fighting to keep from passing out from the lack of oxygen. Just when I thought all was lost, I touched his heel. He was an experienced scuba diver and immediately knew what to do.

I felt him push his mouthpiece into my mouth. I took several deep breaths of the most beautiful air I have ever breathed. While "buddy breathing," we cleared my facemask and slowly made our way to the surface.

We swam toward the beach and our waiting vehicle, all I remember is being wrapped in a wool blanket that was kept in the car for my friend's dog to sleep on. I climbed into the backseat, and he kept the car heater on full blast all the way home.

On Monday morning, I woke up with a bad cold and a fever. Reflecting on what had taken place the day before, I felt a deep sense that God, whoever he was, had played a direct hand in saving my life. Curiosity caused me to search through my stuff for the King James Bible that my mother had given me when I left home. I brushed off the dust and began reading.

"In the beginning God created the heaven and the earth." I got through the first verse. That's not too bad—now all I need to know is when the beginning was.

I got a cup of hot coffee, filled a pipe that Mom had gotten me the Christmas before with Sir Walter Raleigh pipe tobacco, and settled down to continue my journey to find my God.

I ended up with pneumonia and was stuck in bed for the week, but when I wasn't sleeping, I was doing my best to learn to read the Bible. It was grueling work, but I stuck to it. This was new territory. I had to go back and do a lot of re-reading to understand what the verses meant.

As I recovered, I spent every free moment reading the Bible, and the more I read, the better I got.

I learned about Abraham and the covenant that God made with him. I closed my Bible, put it up, and decided to find a religion that would fit my needs. I was going to find myself an Abraham, a prophet that I could identify with from my readings of the old Testament.

I stopped smoking cold turkey. I stopped drinking alcohol and coffee. I flushed my pipe tobacco down the toilet. I dumped a fifth of scotch whiskey, along with a couple of six-packs of beer, down the kitchen drain, and began drinking water, buttermilk, and fruit or vegetable drinks.

One Sunday morning, I called my little sister, Linda, and said that I wanted to start attending church with her, but I wanted to attend a different church every week. After trying out a number of different Christian churches, I couldn't see any difference between them, and I realized what they had in common: the belief that their particular form of religion was better than their neighbor's. Why did they believe that? If all these religions were true, why all the contention and fighting? Between Mrs. Peach, my grandma, and my mom, I had acquired a belief in the fundamentals of Jesus Christ and Christianity. My focus was not so much to find a "true" religion—as interpreted by a group of people who formed a semi-closed social system in which their association was limited to their belief—but rather a religion with a morally conservative environment that would provide me the discipline I needed. I wanted to stand equal to the world in the eyes of society as a whole. I needed an environment that would help me with my inner and outer conflicts, assist me with behavior modification, provide a clear vision to my destiny, and support me in learning. I continued trying one church after another.

Each day, I continued in my efforts to read and understand what I was reading. No matter how slowly I read, I stayed with it. As I slowly began to recognize my inner self and inward challenges, I started to hear that inner voice that we all have and can "tap into" for wisdom.

Finally, I knew which religion to join. It had everything I needed, including new challenges. They expected some sort of donation from their members, which I was more than willing to make, but how? I still had a checking account with $200 in it but no knowledge of how to close it (and I was too proud to go to the bank and ask). A friend showed me how to close the account and retrieve my $200.

I allowed myself to be as humble as wet clay in the master's hands. To keep my perspective and not revert to where I had been, I fasted one twenty-four-hour period each week, often on a different day. When I fasted, I was humble, and as long as I was humble, I remain focused.

An entry from my journal best expresses how I felt:

I walk upon fresh new wet grass;
it smells beautiful under a warm sun.
As heaven increases it's light upon me,
I increase with humble appreciation of my learning.

At church, I met a beautiful young woman named Stella, whom I dated and soon married. I was still working at Bethlehem Steel on the track spike machine when our son was born.

I had a burning desire in my soul to embrace all that I could of this wonderful new world that I was being exposed to. Working the track spike machine had made me strong and fit, and I decided to leave Bethlehem Steel to work in construction as a hod carrier for plaster and brick contractors. The work was heavy and hard but paid well.

I was a slow but steady reader, reading mostly religious works, self-improvement books, and historical novels. I was still using a bastardized form of phonics and, because of the defect in my palate, I struggled with pronunciation. Phonics deals with the repetition of sounds so that learners can identify words, pronounce them correctly, and learn patterns that allow them to learn on their own. My corrupted form of phonics created a "hidden" speech pattern that I could read and learn by, but I could not express myself properly through speech or in written form. Only a few family members, including my sister and new wife, could understand me.

I was determined to make my second family a success, and I had a wonderfully supportive wife. I did not hide my literary struggles from her. She was my "spell checker," dictionary, and English grammar. She was my everything.

We bought a home that was small but affordable, provided I didn't get carried away buying books. I was obsessed by my desire to learn. I absorbed more each day, and I always had a book on my person or stashed in different locations. In later years, my actions reminded me of stories of sea captains who were shipwrecked; those that survived starvation later stashed food, no matter how plentiful it was. I was the same way. No matter where I was, waiting in line or sitting in a doctor's office, I had to have a book with me, a book that challenged me.

One of my favorite places to stash a book was under the front seat of my car—if I were held up due to traffic or road construction, I had something to read. It was also a good place to keep a book secret from my wife. When finances were tight, she tried to rein me in from purchasing more books. She was good at finding my stash, but when she scolded me, it was with a smile that showed that she was more proud than disappointed.

A new world opened up each time I opened a book, but I still could not express myself in written form, a task equally if not more daunting than reading.

17
Defying Odds

In 1969, I was working out of the Hod Carriers Union Hall and waiting to unload the banana boat coming in from Costa Rica. While waiting, I saw in the want ads that the U.S. Secret Service was employing uniformed officers to assist in protecting the president and foreign diplomats. I announced my find to the other union members, and they had a good laugh at the idea of a dumb hod carrier working for the Secret Service.

I was determined to do something more than construction for the rest of my life. I went out to my 1959 Pontiac and got the slacks, shirt, and shoes that I always carried in case such an opportunity for a job interview should arise. As I drove to the Federal Building in Seattle, I wondered what I was doing. Law enforcement? It had always been something to avoid.

The Secret Service? You must be out of your mind! The guys at the Union Hall were right—you've got no business doing what can't be done.

In spite of these thoughts, I knew I had to give it my best shot.

I walked up the steps like I did in Medford with the BLM. This time, I did it with the conviction to be equal with the rest of humanity and to provide the best I could for my wife and children. I walked into the building to find myself among a lot of other men my age. I walked up to the front desk, explained why I was there, and signed in. I was informed that they were issuing entrance exams for the Secret Service Academy within the hour and there would be no other opportunities. This was a one-shot deal.

I retreated into a corner and took stock of the situation.

I don't have a chance. Leave!!! Just walk out and forget about it. If I hurry, I might still be able to catch the banana boat and get the hours I need to get into the stevedore's union. I know from experience that they are only going to hire those who pass in the upper percent, so get out of here!

I couldn't leave. My destiny grabbed me by the balls, and I could not deny it. I leaned back against the wall to observe the environment.

The first thing in my favor was the statement in the paper that said they would accept the GED. I was a Vietnam veteran, and that gave me five extra points on my exam score—if 75 percent was a passing grade, I could make it on 70 percent. My perception of the men around me wasn't encouraging. They could fill the quota with the highest scores, and if a thousand applied and three hundred got 90 percent or better on the exam, they would have first rights.

I dreaded the idea of cheating. If I cheated, I would have a fighting chance of passing this exam, but I really wouldn't be passing.

I moved into survival mode. If the Secret Service was anything like the Navy, the test would be multiple choice. I had to assume that the applicants would be seated in rows, and judging by the number of men I saw, the seating would be close. I had to situate myself strategically when entering the exam room. I moved through the men, and luck was with me. I found exactly what I needed: a cop, left-handed, hopefully smarter than me, and wanting to move up to the Secret Service. All I needed to do was to position myself one row to his right and one seat behind him. This would give me a clear view of his exam sheet.

Like a fog, a familiar, depressing feeling crept over me, just as in the eighth grade when the ancient mariner's albatross returned to "hang so heavy around my neck." I knew that I could not follow through with my plan. I could not violate my own trust in myself.

A dignified-looking man wearing a pinstriped suit came into the room and announced that it was time to take the written portion of the exam. If we passed, we would move on to an oral exam. As we entered the room, my heart leapt. Cubicles. Impossible to copy! Confidence shot through me like a lightning. If I was going to survive this test, I had to stand equal to my fellow man. The exam room was my battleground, my enemy was my First-Grade Life Agreement, and my army was my books.

I picked a cubicle, enclosed on three sides, and looked down at the white Formica tabletop. Chairs shuffled. The clock on the wall read 9:20. The instructor told us that the exam started at 9:30, and we would have one hour to complete it.

In those ten agonizing minutes before the exam, I thought, What is it going to be? To try to pass this test is to fail. To give this your best shot is to fail. You must go further than that—you have to know that you are going to win. To think any less is to lose, and you might as well leave now. Are you going to cheat and fake your way through life? Not this time! Stand up! Evaluate yourself. You can do this!!

The test was put in front of me with the instruction, "Open it and begin."

A calm, confident feeling came over me. My goal could not be denied. I was going to succeed, I knew it as certain as life itself, but not without one hell of a struggle over the next hour.

> Wail not for precious chances passed away!
> Weep not for golden ages on the wane!
> Each night I burn the records of the day-
> At sunrise every soul is born again!
> (Rittenhouse)

I stared at the page, seeing multiple-choice questions dealing with reasoning abilities. Out of four or five choices, I was able to narrow a question down to two and make a good guess. I moved fast, depending on my heart first and my intelligence second.

On the third page, panic hit. Essay questions!

I looked up at the clock, and my soul sank. I was running out of time but could not skip the questions.

Damn! Think, there has to be a way around this. Father in heaven, after all these years, why can't I spell? If you cannot pronounce it, you cannot spell it. Wait, that's the answer—write like a doctor, just run the words together.

As I suspected, they had me clarify some of the essay questions during the oral part of the examination, and I passed the test!

I went home and told my wife the news. She was ecstatic. Everything around me was different. For the first time, I saw myself as equal to those around me. I was a literate man in a literate world! I was the victor of my Armageddon!

My chest was bursting with the joy of accomplishment. I thought of all those who never gave up on me, who accepted me for me, and wrote the following poem, "Cry of the Illiterate."

i walk through this dark wilderness upon a
crooked path many pits there are
dark distasteful

i cry i cry i cry to anyone who will listen to free
me from this wilderness of abandonment

with every fiber of my being I beseech but a
thin sliver of light
Anything to grasp to see to be guided upon
Crowded we are upon this crooked path
engulfed in its cold darkness
with the wind swirling about

i slip i fall upon this path of abandonment i
slide towards a pit where many have fallen
i have faith i have hope i will do it like a young
spring sapling recovering from winter cold
i spring back with each fall my
resilience grows the falls become fewer
so to the pits and turns
then it comes a sliver of discernment from a
great light afar

I grab I try I try i try.................
my head hangs low the pain cuts
my very soul to drag me to my pit of doom my
excuse for failure they were right yes they were
right i stand dumb upon a lonely path my faith
flees from me as a ghost in the night my hope
is lost
they descend upon me jeering
with stench upon their breath
they dance they wave their arms
they are correct charity is not and
ILLITERACY IS MY BONDSMAN

Wait! Wait! I see! Yes; I see a Mother. A
Mother with arms outstretched.

With a tiny spark of will that faith preserved, I
crawl into her waiting arms. She is warm. She
is soft. She is pure as fresh fallen snow.

She pulls me to her breasts.

I CAN READ HER WORDS.

She is called; FAITH, HOPE, CHARITY.

Eight months later, I was in Washington, DC. I took a few days to become situated before reporting to the Secret Service Academy. I was assigned to the second uniformed officers' class referred to as the Executive Protection Service (EPS).

The Department of the Treasury

United States Secret Service Executive Protective Service

This certifies that

Rodney R. Williams

has completed the United States Secret Service Executive Protective Service Recruit Course and is awarded this certificate in recognition of satisfactory completion of all course requirements

Issued at Washington, D.C., this 25th day of September 19 70

Director of Training

Director, U.S. Secret Service

Image 11 Secret Service Academy completion certificate

144

Image 12 My wife snapped this shot of my graduation from the Secret Service Academy (EPS).

18
White House

My first day in the academy was July 13, 1970. President Nixon had arrived the day before and was having breakfast with his staff.

Once in our seats, the instructor drew a pie chart on the chalkboard with a line drawn at the far right, expressing 90 percent and 10 percent. He pointed to the part representing 10 percent of the class and said, "This is the portion of the class that will be assigned to the White House to give direct protection to the president and his immediate family."

I did not take much interest. I figured that I would be in the lower 5 percent of the class, and I had no interest in the White House anyway. I wanted to be on the streets, closer to what I considered my comfort zone.

Four grueling months later, I placed second in my class under the physical fitness program and obtained a 78 percent in academics, which put me in the lower 5 percent of the class. I was recognized as a pistol expert and was assigned to the White House with that 10 percent of the class. I protested but to no avail and was told that I had the profile and physical endurance that made for a good bodyguard. (The 10 percent assigned to the White

House were not necessarily picked for their academic achievements but more for their mental profile.) I assumed that the officer who placed first in physical endurance lacked the right personality type, because he was sent to the streets and I to the White House.

Even though I could classify myself as literate, I was still struggling. I was convinced that I had no short-term memory when it came to numbers, names, rules of grammar, and spelling. We also had a typing class—who thought up this crazy way to scramble the alphabet and stick it on typewriter keys? We were expected to put our fingers on the keyboard and type a report from a scrambled alphabet. I thought that whoever authorized such an insane system should have been fired along with Old King Cole and the fiddlers who hid "g" and "h."

I had been at the White House less than two months when I had my first incident. My assigned post was in the hall near President Nixon's living quarters. Nelson Rockefeller had passed by about an hour earlier to have breakfast with the president.

I saw a tall man with dark brown hair, dressed in a dark blue suit, walking toward me down the hallway. He carried a manila envelope in his left hand, and I noticed that he was not wearing a White House pass. As he approached to pass through the breezeway, I stepped in front of him and asked to see his pass. He said, in an arrogant tone, that he was the president's press secretary and I should know him by sight. I said firmly, "Sir, are you aware that you are to have your White House pass visible at all times? I'm sorry, but I need to see it."

He said, "Officer, I am the president's press secretary. You need to study your photos and know who I am," and attempted to push me aside.

I grabbed him from behind by the belt line and collar of his suit and threw him against the wall, pushed his face against the plush wallpaper with my forearm, and kicked his feet apart. His lips gnarled from the pressure of my forearm, with the skin of his face pushed up around his nose and eyes.

I acted in accordance with my training, which told me that *nothing* was to pass by me unless it fit the parameters of what that post authorized. An unidentified man without proper identification was not within those parameters.

He struggled to get away, dropping the manila envelope stamped CONFIDENTIAL.

"You're under arrest by the authority of the U.S. Secret Service. Anything you say can and will be used against you..."

I heard a noise and turned toward it. About fifty feet away, at the elevator leading to the presidential residence, President Nixon and Nelson Rockefeller stood with surprised looks on their faces. The two Secret Service agents accompanying them motioned for me to release the man.

I obeyed, and Ron Ziegler jerked away from me, shouting that I was fired and he never wanted to see me in the White House again. He marched down the corridor toward President Nixon.

Ironically, I was less afraid of getting fired than about having to type a report of what had just transpired, but the luck of the Irish came to my rescue. The Secret Service is so particular that it did not trust us to write our own reports. I sat down next to a pretty intern who typed the report as I dictated it, edited it, and had me sign it. She told me that G-2 (upper management) edited the part about my physically restraining Mr. Ziegler, presumably because it was embarrassing for him.

Whether you have good luck or not is put to the test when you arrest the president's press secretary. I was fortunate that I didn't find my way back to the Hod Carriers Union. I showed up for duty the next morning expecting that I might be turning in my weapon and badge to be escorted out of the White House. To my surprise, the duty sergeant gave me a big smile and a special acknowledgement of a "job well done" directly from Mr. Youngblood, the assistant director of the Secret Service. I was assigned to the duty post outside Mr. Ziegler's office. Mr. Ziegler wore his White House pass where it could easily be seen and stepped by me with a slight tilt to his head.

I was almost through my probationary year when I received a call to report to administration. The duty officer's words, as best I remember, were, "Officer Williams, in going over your records, we find that you do not have a high school diploma or equivalent." When I said that I had a GED, he replied that I had not had it certified. *What in the ding dong does that mean?* He said I had to present a certified copy before completion of my probationary year or the Secret Service would have no choice but to terminate me.

I went home that evening and asked my wife to explain what *certified* meant. Once I understood, I was relieved. No problem! Just go to the nearest school board and have the GED certified, right?

I went to the Virginia State Department of Education but didn't even get past the receptionist. She looked at the paper and asked, "Are you a resident of the state of Virginia?"

"Yes," I said. Of course I am a resident. I live in Falls Church.

"How long?" she asked with a painted smile.

"Two months."

"I'm sorry, Mr. Williams, that does not qualify for residency in the state of Virginia."

"What do you mean, it doesn't qualify?" I was getting anxious and started leaning across the counter.

She moved away from me slightly. "Sir, you have to be a resident of this state before we can certify your GED."

I was sent to another person who instructed me to contact the school board of the last state I had resided in, Maryland. I had lived there during my academy months and found out that I had never registered with the U.S. Post Office, so I had no evidence of residency there. I called the Washington State Department of Education in Seattle and was told that because I no longer lived there, they could not help and suggested that I contact the state where I took the GED exam. No problem: that would be the best state in the union, my home base, Oregon. Not so good: I was told that I needed to have taken the exam in that state.

By this time, more than a month had elapsed, and I was on a countdown to unemployment. I went back to the Virginia State Department of Education and the receptionist with the painted-on smile. I was in survival mode; this had turned serious. I walked in as if I owned the place, leaned across the counter and returned her smile with my own painted-on smile, presenting my gold-lined Secret Service ID with the presidential seal. "I need to talk to the director. It's very important."

People moved, phones were picked up, and within five minutes, I was in the office of the State Superintendent of Public Instruction. He was a kind man who listened to my story. I realized that by presenting my credentials in this manner for personal reasons, I was putting my job on the line, but there was nothing to lose; it was already on the line. After a couple of stressful weeks, I was notified that under the circumstances, they would make an exception in my case. *Great*, I thought.

That sinking familiar pain of failure and despair came over me again. The State of Virginia would also have to see evidence of my military GED having been certified. I tried to explain that if I had my military GED certification, I would not have to be there.

I had the overwhelming desire to give up and accept failure, a feeling that is hard to describe. Its birth is the nightmare that wakes you, screaming, during the night.

After regaining my composure, I was transferred to another person and told that I would have to retake the GED exam under the direction of the Virginia State Department of Education to receive a certified GED. The receptionist explained that in a couple of months, they would present a series of classes to prepare those taking the test for their GED certificate.

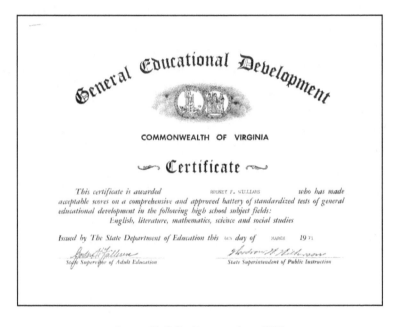

Image 13 I finally *earned* my GED

I explained that I didn't have a couple of months, and she said that it wasn't mandatory to take the classes but it would be helpful if I did. I waived the classes and made arrangements to take my GED exam in two weeks. The words of my grandpa from the banks of the Nehalem River spoke to me: "Refuse to quit, son!"

I took the test and legitimately passed and received my certified GED on March 4, 1971. I was twenty-seven years old and feeling good—God, angels, hard work, and destiny were with me. Many years later, when my wife went through my military records, she came across my U.S. Armed Forces Institute Certification showing that I had successfully completed the USAFI General Educational Development High School Level test. I had cheated to get that satisfactory completion, and somehow misplaced it. It was as though Karma had come full circle, as I know had to earn it the right way. In the end, I made a wrong right, and truth redeemed me.

Dost thou behold thy lost youth all aghast?
Dost reel from righteous Retribution's blow?
Then turn from blotted archives of the past
And find the future's pages white as snow.
(Rittenhouse)

During the 1970s, the Uniformed Branch of the Secret Service was known as the EPS. Whenever a job was posted, you could bid on it according to the number of points that you had earned. I was asked to take the assignment of working President Nixon's hideaway office, located in the Executive Office Building (EOB) across West Executive Avenue from the White House. This surprised me, because this post was favored and held a lot of responsibility, and I had little service time compared to other officers. I accepted my new assignment with enthusiasm and determination to do a good job. Because this was the president's hideaway office, I found myself in direct contact with the president's staff on a daily basis along with senators, congressmen, and movie stars—you name it, they seemed to show up at my desk. President Nixon used this office to conduct private meetings, the organization of the Watergate affair being one of them. He also used it when he wanted to get away from the public and have some solitude.

The back entrance to the EOB office was by way of Executive Avenue, a secure street that was used mostly for White House staff parking. Only those closest to the president were allowed access through this entrance, and a number of these individuals ended up being prosecuted in the Watergate investigation. A sensor that was activated by a pressure pad secured the entrance. Some of President Nixon's staff knew of the sensor and stepped over or around it to enter the reception area unannounced. The staff members I had the biggest problem with were Ron Ziegler, the press secretary, H. R. "Bob" Haldeman, the chief of staff, and Secretary of State Henry Kissinger. Kissinger was worse than the others in that he did not like inconveniences and saw security as a roadblock to be circumvented. He was notorious for showing up unannounced by avoiding the sensor. To correct this, I looked up my favorite White House intern, wrote a memo without mentioning names, and submitted it. Within a short time, a new sensor was installed that prevented

White House staff or anyone else from circumventing the device. The President's staff was not pleased with me and complained but to no avail.

While the President was in his hideaway office, I often shared my post with one or two of the Secret Service Agents assigned to him. We often created mind games to pass the time. On one such occasion, we decided to see who could write all the States of the Union, without looking at a map, in five minutes. The other agents wrote the names of the states in alphabetical order. I wrote them, using an abbreviated form to disguise my spelling, according to their geographic order on the map. When we compared our answers, both agents had missed a few states. When we checked my list, every state was listed correctly in geographic order. Both agents were amazed that I was able to accomplish this. I proudly stated that I could also give them the capitals of all the states, also in geographic order. Both agents were amazed and asked how I learned to do this. I said, "My mom taught me, and I learned."

My wife and I wanted to raise our family in a rural area, preferably on or close to the West Coast. I didn't particularly care for the White House or being a glorified bodyguard, and the notion that I was special because I was around "special" people did not impress me. Life in the White House did not provide enough of the right kind of action.

An interesting opportunity came my way when the Secret Service encouraged EPS officers without a college degree to work toward getting one, especially those who had started college and dropped out. The Secret Service provided incentives. In this way they could pull from their uniform division to fill vacancies among their agents. The officers that took the agency up on the offer were for the most part assigned swing or midnight shifts and allowed to study when not busy. I was encouraged to enroll in the program, obtain a college degree, and receive agent status.

As I brainstormed the idea, I could not see myself being able to accomplish it. I had worked so hard already and barely received a C- in algebra class. I had depended on my five-point veteran status to get me into the Secret Service and graduated academically in the lower 5 percent of my academy class. I couldn't see myself finishing four or five years of college to obtain a bachelor's degree.

My wife and I talked it over. She had faith that if I committed myself, I could do it, but I could not see myself there and chose not to take advantage of the program.

Soon afterward, I had a talk with God.

Father, I need to be challenged, please allow me to learn and advance forward in my life's challenges. I want to give my family the best I can provide for them, but Father, this college stuff is too much for me to handle. I need something simpler. Please provide me with a simpler opportunity to progress and learn. I can only compare college to flying a helicopter to the moon. I can't do it!

I reported for duty and was assigned beside two agents to accompany the president the next day. I found that one of the agents was new and joked with the president in Spanish (few realized that President Nixon spoke Spanish). While performing our duties, I got to talking to this agent and confided in him my desire to remain in some sort of law enforcement but on the West Coast. He asked if I wanted some old-school, cowboy law enforcement action. I was all ears, saying, "Ya betya I do."

He laughed. "You need to go where I came from."

"Where's that?"

"U.S. Border Patrol."

He explained that you didn't have to have a college degree to become a border patrol agent, you just had to pass the entrance exam and get through the academy in Harlington, Texas. The more he talked, the more excited I became.

Before I knew it, I was again at a Federal Building in Washington, DC. I was informed that this exam was "the Treasury Agents exam," and only those scoring 90 percent or better were scheduled for the next class. My heart dropped. *I asked for an easier opportunity, Father, not an equal opportunity. Why would the Border Patrol issue a college-level exam without requiring a college degree?*

To make things even worse, we had to take a language aptitude test. If we passed it, we were given an oral exam, and I was told that only about a third passed.

I segregated everything in my mind to better understand the goal, and that was to pass a college-level exam designed for Treasury agents. If I passed it with a 90 percent or better, I had to take and pass a language aptitude test and then an oral exam, which an average of two-thirds failed. The college was looking better, but I decided to take the Border Patrol entrance exam. If I failed, I still had my position with the Secret Service. Something deep inside told me that what I was getting into was not going to be any easier than getting my college degree.

I showed up as scheduled to take the exam and squeaked by with an 85 percent. With five points for veteran status, I qualified with a 90 percent. I took the language aptitude exam and though I couldn't begin to understand what they wanted from me, I passed.

A week or so later, I showed up for the oral exam. Two criminal investigators dressed in suits, physically fit and intimidating, sat across the table from me. The first question caught me by surprise. It went somewhat like this: "You are stationed at the U.S.-Canadian border, and you are about to check train passengers for proper authorization to enter the United States. You have received intelligence that eight Chinese nationals are being smuggled with altered or counterfeit immigration documents, and the smuggler is with them. You are limited in the time that you can hold the train. You have two minutes to answer how you would identify and apprehend the illegal aliens along with their smuggler."

Both agents folded their hands and stared across the table at me with demanding looks. I started sweating bullets. I stared back as my mind raced to come up with an acceptable process, hoping they would let up on the unnerving stare.

Looking at one and then the other, I finally gave my answer. "Sir, I would look for eight Chinese Nationals sitting together…"

"They're not sitting together. They're scattered throughout the train," an agent said, leaning slightly toward me.

I regained my composure as best I could. "I would go through the train and gather together the eight Chinese Nationals and…."

The other agent interrupted, impatiently glancing at his wristwatch. "There are more than eight ethnic Chinese on the train; there are twenty ethnic Chinese on the train." He emphasized *ethnic* as if giving me a hint.

I took a deep breath and continued. "I would gather up all twenty ticket stubs from the ethnic Chinese, find the numeric sequence of eight ticket stubs, and segregate those eight from the rest."

"One of the woman passengers is accusing you of being prejudiced for singling out the Chinese. You need to hurry. You're about out of time."

"Sir, I would apologize and continue checking the numeric sequence of the ticket stubs. I would then segregate those eight for further questioning. Once they had been determined, I would go back to those that I had segregated as the possible smuggler and check the passenger with the preceding ticket number and the passenger with the following ticket number."

"Why would you do that?" an agent asked.

"Because, Sir, logic tells me that the smuggler would purchase the tickets for the illegal Chinese and then purchase his own, thus having a preceding or following ticket number. This narrows the possible suspects down to two."

We went through several more similar questions before they asked the last one. "You're on the U.S.-Mexican border. You have a fence defining the border. You observe a man, a woman, and an infant cross the border through a hole in the fence. You give chase and apprehend the father and infant, but the mother escapes back into Mexico. What are you going to do?"

"I would load up the father and child and transport them back to the station for processing."

One of the agents stood, leaned across the table, and stated, "The mother is screaming that she nurses her baby, and the baby cannot survive without her milk." The agent leaned into my face. "What are you going to do? She's screaming her head off. She's making a scene. What are you going to do, Agent Williams? Tell me now!"

"I would call for backup."

"You can't, your radio is dead."

Both agents demanded quick answers, and after several more attempts, I said, "I would secure the father, take the infant back to the border fence, hand it to its

160

mother, and then transport the father to the station for processing."

Both agents yelled, "Are you telling us that you would return an illegal alien back across an international border without direction from your superiors? Is that what you are telling us, Agent Williams?"

"Yes sir. I had no communication to receive any other direction, and the infant was only a victim of its parents' actions. I would not risk the infant's life."

Both agents smiled, shook my hand, and asked me to wait outside for a few minutes. After a short while, I was called back in and told that I had been accepted into the U.S. Border Patrol Academy. I would be notified when the academy would start and whether my first duty station would be El Paso, Texas, or Chula Vista, California.

On March 7, 1972, the day my wife gave birth to our third child, a baby girl, I was informed that I had been accepted into the next border patrol class and was assigned to Chula Vista.

19
Border Patrol

My wife and I were excited about being in Southern California and the adventure before us. I had just enough time to get my family situated and report to the Chula Vista Sector, and was then on my way to the academy.

My lovely wife was there to see me off to yet another Federal law enforcement academy. This time, I was required to have a working knowledge of Spanish in five and a half months. If I failed this, I was out, gone, *afuera, no mas*. As my wife kissed me goodbye at the boarding platform, she slipped a note into my shirt pocket.

I found my seat on the plane and waved to my family members standing in the terminal. As soon as we got into the air, I reached into my shirt pocket to read what I was certain to be a love note but instead saw *A verb is— A noun is— A preposition is— An adjective is—*

The list went on, giving the definitions. She closed with *I love and believe in you.*

The full realization of what I had gotten myself into began to sink in with a vengeance. I was on my way to one of the toughest law enforcement academies. I would have to learn and apply immigration law and naturalization law and do it all in a foreign language in five and a half months. The weight of it all fell upon me. I leaned back and put my hands over my face. *Oh my Father, my God, what have I done? What have I done? I have thrown away the most secure job a man could ask for. The benefits, retirement, prestige of protecting the President of the United States of America, the security for my wife and children. Oh my Father, what have I done?*

The stewardess interrupted my thoughts, asking if I would like a refreshment. I nodded and turned to look out the window. Below I could make out what I guessed was the Southern Pacific freight strung out like a long snake, "highballing" across the desert. Tears welled in my eyes, and I again felt a yearning for the freedom of the hobo.

Why me, Lord? Why me? If only I could be down there hoboin with my friends on a cannonball across the country side. Free as the wind, yes, born the next of kin, the next of kin to the wayward wind, with the gypsy spirit deep within my soul. Junglin-up at some railroad interchange next to a warm fire smoking snipes, drinkin hobo coffee an eatin bullets, all the time a-tellin yarns about the places I'd been, da people I'd seen, da things I'd done. Why me Lord, why me?

The words of Walter Malone's poem "Opportunity" came to me again:

> They do me wrong who say I come no more
> When once I knock and fail to find you in;
> For every day I stand outside your door
> And bid you wake, and rise to fight and win.
>
> (Rittenhouse)

My flight landed in some large city in Texas, where I met with several other men headed for the Border Patrol Academy. We transferred to a smaller plane and headed for the academy. I saw fields of cotton and flatland shaped by small, rolling hills of mesquite brush. The locals referred to them as trees, but where I came from, they were bushes at best. We arrived at the academy, were shown around, and were taken to our barracks. We were assigned to a room that consisted of two beds and a single desk. A bathroom and shower area were down the hall, in the middle of the barracks floor. *Welcome home. You are now Trainee Williams and will remain such for the next ten months.*

The classes were divided into two parts: half the day learning Spanish and the other half learning immigration and naturalization law.

At 7:00 a.m. sharp, I showed up for class and nervously took my seat. Our Spanish instructor came in, silently looked us over, smiled, and turned to write on the blackboard, "Mi nombre es Carlos Armendaris Gutierrez." He turned to the class and used a pointer to identify what he had written. "Your first assignment is to memorize my name, pronounce it correctly, and write it correctly. You will be tested on this tomorrow morning when class begins. Every day you will be tested on what you were given to learn the day before. Each Friday you will be tested on what you were given to learn during that week, and each month you will be tested on the previous month's assignments. Your final exam will be given on the morning of your last day. If you are caught cheating, you will be immediately terminated. Do you understand?"

We all said, "Yes, Sir."

I looked at the name and listened to my instructor pronounce it over and over.

Here I sit, having been given a larynx the same as the rest of humanity, but I can't even pronounce the English language, and now look what I have to do, and spell it on top of that? Oh my, Oh my, Mistress Mary, quite contrary, how does your garden grow? With silver bells and cockle shells, and pretty maids all in a row. Oh my, Oh my, it's only been a few years since I have been able to spell my own middle name, and now I have to do what? Not only pronounce it but also spell what? Sorry folks, dead man walking here.

That evening, I and several others from my class got together with a few of the Mexican-American trainees and practiced pronouncing our instructor's name. To my amazement, I found that by breaking the name down into syllables and repeating them with my classmates, I was able to pronounce his name as well as they were. We printed the syllables over and over.

The next morning when entering Spanish class, we were nervous but ready. We all did it! Mr. Carlos Armendaris Gutierrez was not an extraterrestrial from some far-off galaxy after all. We pronounced his name correctly and, when called upon, spelled it correctly. At the end of the class, he smiled as if to say, "See, that wasn't so bad after all, was it?"

We were then tested on our knowledge of English grammar, which I failed miserably. I found myself with a few other trainees in a quick-start class, and we were told that we needed to understand basic English grammar if we expected to learn Spanish grammar. Our class was small, and we got one-on-one attention from the instructor and his assistants. At day's end, we formed study circles to review the work, which helped tremendously on the next day's test.

It wasn't long before I noticed that with my limited vocabulary, I was able to speak and write Spanish quite well. Immigration law was another thing. Having never been required to do homework and learn proper study habits, I found myself at the same disadvantage as when at the Secret Service Academy. My fellow trainees got their homework done and then had spare time, especially on weekends.

I spent my weekends studying. I walked into the desert, smelling the chaparral (dwarf oaks) and mesquite, to find a shady place to study. There in its silent solitude, I was content with my studies. I spoke Spanish to those who would listen: the desert squirrels, tarantulas, tortoises, and on a few occasions, rattlesnakes. During the week, I studied from early evening to midnight, and it paid off.

The first part of the academy lasted four and a half months, and during that time, I left the academy grounds only twice. My Spanish instructor encouraged us to go into the border town, Brownsville, and practice speaking Spanish with the local merchants.

I went into town to purchase a pair of dress boots that were popular among the Border Patrol agents. As I went into a merchandise store that was popular with the agents, I was nervous about my first attempt to speak Spanish beyond the academy. A pretty sales girl greeted me, and I couldn't help but wonder what she thought as I shifted my weight and finally got up the nerve to ask in Spanish about buying a pair of boots.

She cocked her head and answered in English. "I'm sorry, I didn't understand what you asked. You're from the Border Patrol Academy, aren't you?"

Relieved, I confessed that I was and repeated my question in English.

She laughed and put me at ease by using a slow-paced, second- to third grade-level Spanish and directing me to the area of the store that had what I needed. I was impressed that I could understand some of what she said. I purchased a brand new pair of boots and wore them out of the store.

In 1970 Brownsville, every other street corner had a shoeshine boy, eight to twelve years old, carrying a portable shoeshine kit. I decided that my new boots needed a shine, so I confidently approached one lad and boldly blurted what I thought meant that I wanted him to shine my new boots, "Yo quiero una bezuda."

The poor lad gave me a horrible look of fright and took off running as fast as he could.

A few months later, I went back into town, wearing the boots, to purchase a hat. I saw a different shoeshine boy on the corner, approached him, and asked for his services, this time in English. While he was shining my boots, I asked him how to say *shoeshine* in Spanish.

"Betunada, yo quiero betunada," he said.

I thought about what I had said my first time in town when I asked for a shoeshine. "Young man, what does *bezuda* mean?"

He answered with a laugh. "Sir, that means a woman with a big fat lip or a kiss, depending how you use it." Putting his free hand next to his lower lip, he made a "fat lip," saying "Bezuda."

I couldn't help but laugh. I had asked the first lad if he wanted "to kiss my boot"—no wonder he ran away, as well he should have. I was lucky that he didn't get his dad to beat me up or call the police.

I graduated from the first part of the academy, grateful for a passing grade, but it wasn't over. In a month and a half, I would be tested again on immigration and naturalization law and a working command of Spanish at my assigned station, Chula Vista. I could not afford to relax. I spent all my free time studying flash cards on Immigration and Naturalization Service (INS) law and Spanish. After my shift was over, I went to the detention center, picked up a pack of cigarettes and a Coke, and watched one of the older *campesinos* who had recently been arrested and was awaiting transport back to Mexico or Central America. I took him into the desert, sat him down, gave him the Coke and a cigarette, and practiced my pronunciation and sentence structure. I pointed at objects and asked, "Como se dice?"

My five-and-a-half month exam was presented in two parts: INS law and Spanish. I did average on the INS law and dreaded the Spanish part of the exam, because I had heard many stories of trainees failing and getting a one-way ticket home. I would have to write the answers in both Spanish and English.

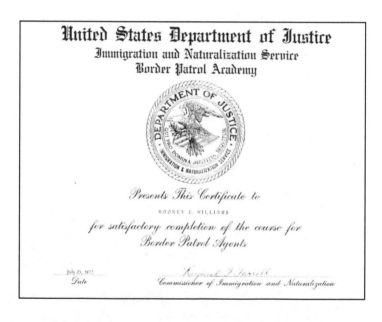

United States Department of Justice
Immigration and Naturalization Service
Border Patrol Academy

Presents This Certificate to

RODNEY F. WILLIAMS

for satisfactory completion of the course for
Border Patrol Agents

July 25, 1972
Date

Raymond F. Farrell
Commissioner of Immigration and Naturalization

Image 14 Border Patrol Academy completion certificate

I walked into the exam room, in full dress uniform and an ache in my stomach, and met two senior patrol agents. They gave me, in English, a scenario of an illegal alien being questioned. One of the agents acted the part of the illegal alien, and I was to question him by translating English question to Spanish. If he understood me, he answered in Spanish, and I wrote his answer in English under the question that I had just translated to him. I understood what was being said but was not able to write it properly in English. The bottom line was that I had learned the basics of English grammar but still could not spell. I compensated by reverting to my doctor-chicken-scratch that I had successfully used when taking the entrance exam to the Uniform Branch of the Secret Service. Then everything was reversed, and I had to write English to Spanish translations.

When the test was complete, I was told that I had passed the INS law portion with an 82 percent. The Spanish test was pass or fail.

Image 15 My Border Patrol Class, 1972

I was told something like this: "Agent Williams, your conversational Spanish was acceptable, but we had a difficult time understanding your written English answers. Your penmanship is barely readable but readable. On the other hand, your Spanish penmanship was fine and easy to read and understand. Other than a few grammar mistakes, you did fine. As a matter of fact, you did not misspell a single Spanish word."

Great, I passed!

After that exam, we had to start writing our own incident reports. Old habits die hard—I could not spell! I carried a spell-check dictionary everywhere I went. When writing my reports, I often could not spell well enough to find the word in Webster's dictionary. When that happened, I tried to call my wife, and if that was not possible, my best guess had to do. It wasn't long before my Senior Patrol Agent (SPA) cautioned me that my bad spelling would reflect upon my evaluations for advancement. He suggested that I do extra writing at home; I should write a book and have my wife critique it for me.

I did just that. My first book was *A La Brava*, a wonderful story about a young man from Guatemala coming to the United States illegally to find his dream of a better life. This did not help much with my spelling. While my Spanish phonics were fine, my English phonics were not.

During my employment with the Border Patrol, I came to know the campesinos. They were peasants and farm labors, better known in the United States as migrant workers. They harvested crops from season to season and from border to border with an unspoken understanding that they would be paid for their labor. The majority of the illegal alien arrests along the Mexican border were campesinos.

When I arrested the campesinos and questioned them about their citizenship and how they entered the United States, I realized that I was often dealing with illiteracy that was passed on from generation to generation. They couldn't read the report that I filled out or sign it with any knowledge of what had just transpired. They had to accept my word, and their struggle to understand the proper Spanish that I had been taught in the academy was as great as my struggle to understand their slang.

I had to adapt to understand what I was dealing with. When a campesino made a statement such as "Lo sentimos, Senor, somos no mas que pollos y pagamos el coyote dinero y el nos llevo a un pollero que nos guio hasta la linea y brincamos a la

Image 16 A new Border Patrol rookie, standing with my baby girl.

172

brava," it roughly translated, "We're sorry, sir. We are just chickens and paid the coyote money, and he gave us to a chicken herder who guided us to the line, and we jumped bravely."

I was understand-ably confused. Why would chickens pay a coyote to be given to a chicken herder? Coyotes steal chickens from the chicken herder, not give them chickens, and what is this line that they are jumping bravely across? The language of the campesinos fleeing across our border from Mexico opened my eyes to a new subculture of language, reminding me of my days with the hoboes. I quickly adapted to speak at a level they could understand.

In 1974, I was involved in a court case involving an illegal teenaged campesino who had been kidnapped. The court translator had been educated in Madrid and had degrees in Spanish and English. No matter the excellent command that she had of both languages, she could not understand the slang of the young man, nor could he understand her. The judge asked, "Does anyone in the court understand this young man?"

One of the Border Patrol agents said, "Yes, I do."

The judge called the agent before the court and had him speak to the young man. He understood the agent perfectly, and the trial proceeded with the agent acting as court translator.

The language of the campesino was tied to the illiterate world that was close to mother earth, not to the logical, technological world of the literate. His language was the raw behavior of nature—the relationship of the coyote to the chicken and the line in the desert that he would have to jump over instead of a border that he would legally cross. His speech was a language of survival first and convenience second.

They were but a step behind me. I was once as they were, understood by few. Along with many Border Patrol agents, I had compassion and respect for the illiterate campesinos and treated them with understanding. A few agents mistreated the campesinos, and sadly, biased news reporters gave attention to them.

Why do we have so many of these campesinos flooding across our borders, risking their lives and the lives of their children to join the millions of illegal aliens already in our country? The answer is simple. Americans enjoy by birthright or legal immigration the greatest opportunities on the planet. Respected poet Emma Lazaruz of New York, a reader and dreamer, was troubled by the violent injustices suffered by Jews in Eastern Europe, and she wrote, "The New Colossus," known as "Your Huddled Masses," of which the last five lines can be found on the Statue of Liberty.

> *Not like the brazen giant of Greek fame*
> *With conquering limbs astride from land to land;*
> *Here at our sea-washed, sunset gates shall stand*
> *A mighty woman with a torch, whose flame*
> *Is the imprisoned lightning, and her name*
> *Mother of Exiles. From her beacon-hand*
> *Glows world-wide welcome; her mild eye command*
> *The air-bridged harbor that twin cities frame,*
> *"Keep, ancient lands, your storied pomp!" cries she*

With silent lips. "Give me your tired, your poor,
Your huddled masses yearning to breathe free,
The wretched refuse of your teeming shore,
Send these, the homeless, Tempest-tossed to me,
I lift my lamp beside the golden door!"
(Lazarus)

The campesinos' life agreement gives them two alternatives: stay in Mexico and accept poverty or escape to America and make their life more tolerable.

One warm sunny day while patrolling the east side of San Ysidro, I looked over a freshly harvested field of tomatoes next to a high fence that marked the U.S.-Mexico border. I had just picked a bag of ripe tomatoes to take home to my wife, and I knew from experience that the campesinos would soon come to glean what was left over from the harvest. I also knew that the *contrabandistas* (drug smugglers) often used the campesino as cover to smuggle marijuana across the border. I was waiting for them.

I wrote the following poem in memory of what transpired that afternoon.

The Hellish Thing
it shines under hot desert sun
strands of steel, tight and strong run west to east
rusty barbs rolled in corals to adorn her lofty heights
red, blue, green cloth from shirt, blouse, pants

cling to those rusty barbs
evidence of one's brave challenge past
yearning to breathe free

the golden door is closed!
the lamp is out!
it is a dismal sight, for hope is lost
it is a Hellish Thing!

the emptiness of ages past haunts her brown face
on her shoulders the burden of the campesino
both rapture and despair accompany her stride
two children follow close behind

the wind
she sings a ghostly tune
it gently touches the lice infested hair
lifting it up
the children cling to their mother's side
what breath blew out the lights within their little
hearts

time's tragedy is in the their aching stare
to fruitful fields afar
plundered, profaned, disinherited are they
their cry is protest to the powers
a protest that is prophecy fulfilled

the mother speaks
"go my daughter to the fruitful field
look! There is a hole in the fence to pass"
"but mother," pleads the young girl
"we dare not cross, surly La Migra waits in the
shadows"
"do not worry, go! And take Juanito with you
fear not La Migra
for he will see your innocence so pure
I cannot follow for my innocence is masked by my
years"

the journey was long
our cupboard reaps not
waiting for our return

a dollar was spent for the torn dress you wear
a dollar is not left to fill the stomach of Juanito

wait not, look!
the tomatoes are red and plump
hewn down, discarded, laid to waste
it is but a stone's throw away
hurry for the day grows long

take this pail, this box
let them be filled with the wasteful riches
of the Nortenos
be on your way obey!

large brown eyes give witness to the fear
that grips the very soul of the little girl
she takes her brother's hand

he follows, he looks back at his Mama
there is an ache within him
he knows not its meaning
in faith he allows his sister to lead him

the barbs they grab hold of his blue shirt stopping him
mama comes to her son to free the shirt
a part is torn loose, left, Juanitos signature
to be spoken by natures wind

La Migra, having watched, comes from the shadows
his majestic power with shining steel
flashing red and blue lights wailing siren
dominates all

mama screams
a mournful scream from deep within her soul
she runs to the fence

the young girl looks up from her labor
the fear of millions past grips her tender breast
she trembles and weakens unable to answer mama's
call

Juanito with fearful eyes looks on in terror
first to mama then to his sister
he is caught betwixt the two
the fearful outcast in dirty rags knows not which way
to run

it is too late
La Migra descends upon his pray
like a cheetah to the gazelle
the steel monster slides to a stop
with black tires locked in a cloud of dust

La Migra disembarks from his shining monster
he stands straight and tall
he looks around to see but three

what power this Migra giant has
to make any escape appear
like the feeble wave of a baby's fist against a storm
there is no gift to give

La Migra beckons the girl to come
she fears him greatly
she knows not what to do
her rags will not cover sufficient her skin so bear

but wait! What is this!
La Migra bids Juanito to help his sister

La Migra takes the pail and fills it full
"fear not little ones for I shall fill the box, too"

he takes them the stone's throw
where mama waits trembling in fear
and gives forth the much needed food

then…………………
he reaches through the fence
across the border of two Nations

mama, she fears his reach to flinch a bit…….then
with his thumb that has held the hammer of many
guns
he tenderly wipes a tear from beneath her eye
from his wallet he hands her money and speaks
"fear not little mother for God is the Master"

mama, she divides the load amongst the three
it is four miles home
to a cupboard that will reap well

La Migra stands arrayed in green against a desert sea
to gaze upon a piece of blue cloth caught on barbed
steel

the three they turn and leave
bowed down by the weight of harvest left
no voice do they impart

180

La Migra having once turned round walks away
to turn no more his head
a silent friend he knows
doth beside him tread

20
What Now?

A dillar, a dollar, a ten o'clock scholar
What makes you come so soon?
You used to come at ten o'clock
But now you come at noon!
(Bjoland)

Image 17 Ten O'Clock Scholar

In addition to apprehending and processing people who crossed the border illegally, we often processed INS petitions from people who were applying to legally enter the United States. This is when I became intimate with INS how-to procedures as opposed to the "catch and release" quagmire of "how not to." This experience was another steppingstone for my future.

After spending eight years with the Border Patrol, working both Mexican and Canadian borders, I decided to pursue private employment. I used my experience in Federal law enforcement to secure employment as the head of security for a large church-owned enterprise and later to start a consulting business that helped businesses and people navigate U.S. immigration procedures. This led me to writing two books on how to immigrate to the United States.

My greatest fear in overcoming illiteracy was that I would pass my struggles along to my children. When entering the fifth grade, our daughter, Kelly, was found to be reading at a third-grade level. Her teacher told us that she would be graded at fifth-grade standards. To help Kelly read better, she was assigned to special education classes.

It wasn't long before she started acting out. She came home from school and complained that she saw herself as a retard. Her mother had her pulled from her special education class, started working directly with the school administrators to have her professionally tested, and saw that an advocate was assigned to work with her. Within a few years, Kelly caught up with the rest of her class and completed high school. Today, she is the mother of four children, married to a schoolteacher, and runs a part-time business from her home.

One of my sons, when entering the fifth grade, started showing similar learning disabilities. One day, when his mother attempted to read his notes from an interview that he had conducted for a class project, she was not able to understand them. When I saw his notes, I was alarmed to see that, like me, he was creating his own improvised style of writing.

His mother went to the school administrators, and not satisfied with what they offered, we decided to get specialized help outside of the school district. We hired a recognized professional who specialized in identifying learning disabilities to diagnose our son. Along with a new learning curriculum, her diagnosis was submitted to the school, and an individual learning plan was implemented. He went on to become president of the school's honor society and to attend college with a major in environmental science.

When our children started school, we were involved in their learning. We chose to educate them in the public schools, but we did not leave the responsibility of teaching solely in the hands of the school administrators. We used the system as a support for their education as a whole. We have a family saying, "Home schooling 101, Daddy style."

My mother read to me from *The Child's World*, my grandma sang and recited nursery rhymes to me, my grandpa threw me into the Nehalem river that chilly day and counseled me on life's lessons, and my abusive stepdad taught me to defend myself. Where would I be today had they "tried" to read to me or "tried" to sing to me, or "tried" to throw me into the river, or "tried" to teach me to defend myself? Parents are the front-line educators of their children, and life's lessons are not built on trying. I had been chiseled from rough granite, and it wasn't done by trying.

When my son, David, turned fourteen, his mother and I ended up in a custody battle. When I was illiterate and going through a divorce, I was unable to express myself. Not this time. I was now able to address myself, both orally and in writing, well enough to show the court that I was worthy to have custody of my son.

Over the last fifty years, education has evolved from educating only those who qualify to "no child left behind." I was unable to complete the eighth grade and dropped out of high school, but in spite of my First-Grade Life Agreement and the educational system, I have succeeded in becoming literate and forged to a successful career.

Today, as a father and one who has fought the battle to overcome illiteracy, I ask myself, *How can I make a difference?* I read in a study that out of twenty high-income countries, the United States ranks twelfth on literacy.

Why are only 50 percent of Americans able to read above the eighth-grade level? Why are 20 percent of Americans functionally illiterate and reading below a fifth-grade level? Why is it that 30 million Americans cannot read a simple sentence?

Does illiteracy affect our society? Yes! Three out of five inmates in American prison systems cannot read. Seventy percent of prisoners fall into the lowest two levels of reading proficiency, and 80 percent of juvenile offenders have problems reading. Approximately 50 percent of Americans are unable to read well enough to balance a checkbook or read a prescription drug label, and some states base the number of prison beds needed upon elementary students' reading tests.

Fifty years ago, the family unit in general was strong, and the educational system was weak. Today, while the educational system has made marked improvements, the family as a unit has steadily declined. This leaves too many children, and adults, in the claws of illiteracy. When families and educators come together, children succeed. Each link of the chain—parent, child, and teacher—must function in harmony for overall success. When a teacher gives up on a child, the parent must pick up the slack to help the child find a different teacher or a better way of learning.

I know teachers who are challenged with children who barely get by in class because they are exposed at home to neglect, abuse, alcohol, and drugs. Administrators are faced with budget crises and overcrowding, resulting in avoidance of Individual Education Plans (IEPs). Children fall through the cracks or are given mind-numbing drugs to subdue their naturally curious, and sometimes objectionable, behavior.

Some children cope in other ways: drugs, sex, alcohol, and suicide.

On the other hand, I know parents who are furious with school administrators and teachers for failing to provide their children the tools to achieve successful grades. Some parents turn to homeschooling out of a distrust of the school system, fear that their children will become corrupted by children with lesser values, or both. There are the arguments about the homeschooled child's ability to socialize outside of the home environment; the notion is that the only place to learn socially acceptable behavior is by interacting with others at school. I wanted to live "outside the box" of society to avoid academic failure, but had I been allowed to give into this desire, I would likely have never become literate.

Options for parents are there for some but not all. For instance, in Washington State, homeschooling can be done only if the parent is able to (1) be supervised by a certificated teacher for one contact hour per week, (2) have earned forty-five college-level credit hours or one year of college, (3) be deemed sufficiently qualified to homeschool by the superintendent of the school district of residence, or (4) have completed a course in home-based instruction at a post-secondary institution or vocational-technical school.

In other states, parents are branded "rednecks" if they choose homeschooling, and some must fight with local government agencies for the privilege. Private schools are often a good option but only if the family can afford the steep tuition. Since the 1990s, charter schools have become a viable option, where parents are accountable for their children's education while still receiving the benefits of public school funding. However, not every state offers charter schools; ten states are still fighting to pass legislation to allow them.

Charles Dickens stated that "my satire is against those who see figures and averages, and nothing else" (Dickens). The parodies that he created about the strict analytical thinkers of society lead to his classic novel *Hard Times*, in which Thomas Gradgrind, a "fanatic of the demonstrable fact," is the protagonist. The word *fact*, which Mr. Gradgrind uses liberally, can be replaced with the word *reality*. For in my case, reality was the deciding fact.

Accepting reality is the only way to stop the "snowball from racing down the hill" when a child is screaming for help. Parents and educators must come together. Allowances must be made for each child, each family, and each school. All parties involved must take on an attitude of cooperation and determination. If one person in the link becomes apathetic, the results can be devastating.

When my First-Grade Life Agreement was unwittingly determined by my administrators and reinforced by family and friends, what did I do? I thought, *You want me to be a Simple Simon, I'll be a Simple Simon just for you.* As the judgment was repeated and forced upon me, I came to believe it. My saving grace was my mother reading to me and my sister, Peggy, helping me to understand and translating my attempts at writing. Of course, my strongest advocates were my grandparents, especially my grandpa. My heart supported these influences and would not abandon me. That strength within me would not give into judgment.

Remember Simple Simon?

Simple Simon went a-fishing
For to catch a whale;
But all the water he could find
Was in his mother's pail.

(Bjoland)

Every child looks for a "whale" but often is provided only a pail of water. We owe our children every opportunity that can be provided for them.

In the spring of 1982, I visited the King County Library in Renton, Washington. Twenty years earlier in 1962, when entering the base library at the naval base in Yokosuka, I did so with hesitation, but this time I had a purpose. I walked through the front doors confidently, smiled at the lady behind the information desk, and briskly walked to the how-to section.

There it was, *How to Immigrate without a Lawyer* by Rod Williams, just as my publisher had said it would be. I pulled the copy off the shelf and stood for a long moment, holding it. The book was alive, even more alive than *The Wahoo Bobcat* had been so many years before. A warm, confident feeling of accomplishment came over me. I walked to a reading area to make myself comfortable in one of the chairs. I gazed at the cover and gently caressed it as a parent would a child. I opened it to read the opening words: "Would you go to a brain surgeon for a headache? Would you buy a world atlas to find your way to the next town? Would (or should) you hire an expensive attorney to tell you what you can learn for yourself by just reading a book?"

Tears of joy filled my eyes. I heard myself say as if from a distance, "I can, and I did!"

Simple Simon went a-fishing
for to catch a whale;
Simple Simon caught his whale
and now bids you all adieu.

Works Cited

Aires, Philip. *Centuries of Childhood, A Social History of Family Life*. New York: Jonathan Cape Ltd, 1962.

Aristotle. *ASL Info.com*. http://www.aslinfo.com/trivia.html (accessed Feb 10, 2012).

Banzahaf, Hajo. *Tarot and the Journey of the Hero*. York Beach, ME: Samuel Weiser, Inc.

Bjoland, Esther M. *Stories of Childhood, The Child's World in Six Volumes, Volume One*. Chicago: The Child's World, Inc., 1950.

Coleridge, Samuel Taylor. *The Literature Network*. http://www.online-literature.com/coleridge/646/ (accessed Feb 10, 2012).

Dickens, Charles. *Hard Times*. New York: Simon and Schuster, 2007.

Gillilan, Strickland. *Your Daily Poem*. http://www.yourdailypoem.com/listpoem.jsp?poem_id=352 (accessed Feb 10, 2010).

Hale, Edward E. *The Project Gutenberg Ebook of The Man Without a Country and Other Tales*. 2005. http://en.wikipedia.org/wiki/The_Man_Without_a_Country (accessed Feb 10, 2012).

Lazarus, Emma. *Wikipedia*. http://en.wikipedia.org/wiki/The_New_Colossus (accessed Feb 10, 2012).

Rittenhouse, Jessie B. *The Little Book of American Poets: 1787-1900*. Cambridge: Riverside Press, 1915.

Tildsley, John L. *The Mounting Waste of the American Secondary School*. Cambridge: Harvard University Press, 1936.

Unknown. *Poetry Foundation*. http://www.poetryfoundation.org/poem/171643 (accessed Feb 10, 2012).